ROYAL COURT

LOYAL WOMEN

by Gary Mitchell

First performance at the Royal Court Jerwood Theatre Downstairs,
Sloane Square, London on 5 November 2003.

LOYAL WOMEN

by **Gary Mitchell**

Cast in order of appearance
Rita **Valerie Lilley**
Brenda **Michelle Fairley**
Jenny **Lisa Hogg**
Mark **Mark McCrory**
Gail **Clare Cathcart**
Maureen **Julia Dearden**
Heather **Cara Kelly**
Terry **Stephen Kennedy**
Adele **Sinéad Keenan**

Director **Josie Rourke**
Designer **Christopher Oram**
Lighting Designer **David Plater**
Sound Designer **Ian Dickinson**
Assistant Director **Elizabeth Freestone**
Assistant to Designer **Paul Wills**
Casting **Lisa Makin**
Production Manager **Paul Handley**
Stage Manager **Marion Marrs**
Deputy Stage Manager **Sarah Waling**
Assistant Stage Manager **Linsey Hall**
Costume Supervisor **Iona Kenrick**
Fight Director **Richard Ryan**
Dialect Coach **Majella Hurley**
Company Voice Work **Patsy Rodenburg**
Set built by **Rupert Blakeley**

The Royal Court Theatre would like to thank the following for their help with this production:

THE COMPANY

Gary Mitchell (writer)

For the Royal Court: The Force of Change, Trust.
Other theatre includes: Deceptive Imperfections
(Belfast Festival/Traverse); As the Beast Sleeps
(National Theatre Society/Abbey, Dublin/Lyric,
Belfast/Tricycle); Marching On (Lyric, Belfast/7.84
Theatre Company); Energy (Playhouse,
Londonderry); Tearing the Loom (Lyric, Belfast);
In A Little World of Our Own (Abbey, Dublin/Lyric,
Belfast/Donmar); Sinking, That Driving Ambition
(Replay Theatre Company).
Film and television includes: Suffering (BBC
Northern Ireland), As the Beast Sleeps (BBC
Northern Ireland/BBC 2), An Officer from France
(RTE), Red, White and Blue (BBC 1), Made in
Heaven (BBC).
Radio includes: Drumcree, Poison Hearts,
Independent Voice, The World, The Flesh and the
Devil (BBC Radio 4), Stranded (BBC Radio 3).
Awards include: Charles Wintour Most Promising
Playwright Award 2000 for The Force of Change,
joint winner of the George Devine Award 2000 for
The Force of Change, Belfast Arts Award for Best
Short Film for Suffering (which Gary also directed),
Belfast Arts Award Best Film for As the Beast
Sleeps, Pearson Best Play Award 1999 for Trust,
Irish Times Theatre Award for Best New Play 1997
and Belfast Arts Drama Award 1998 for In a Little
World of Our Own, Belfast Arts Drama Award
1998 for Sinking, Stewart Parker Award 1994 for
Independent Voice, BBC Radio 4 Young Playwrights
Festival Award for The World, the Flesh and the
Devil.

Clare Cathcart

Theatre includes: Aristocrats (Chichester Festival
Theatre); Gone to L.A (Hampstead); Romeo and
Juliet (Greenwich); After the Rain (Gate);
The Party's Over (Nottingham Playhouse);
Translations (Donmar); Fooling About, Venetian
Twins (Oxford Stage Company); Cloud Nine,
The Duchess of Malfi (Contact, Manchester);
Same Old Moon (Globe); Joyriders (Tricycle).
Television includes: Ultimate Force, Wired, Sins,
I Saw You, Strangerers, Psychos, Hambone's Day,
Mature Adults, Sunny's Ears, Accused, Kiss and Tell,
Coronation Street, Safe and Sound, The Bill,
Casualty, Over Here, Searching, Father Ted,
Goodnight Sweetheart, Alexei Sayle Show,
Inspector Alleyn, Rides, Lovejoy, Murder Most
Horrid, Perfect Scoundrels, Lost Belongings.
Film includes: Cor Blimey, Breathtaking, Secret
Society, Salvage, Hotel Sordide, Up on the Roof,
Amazing Grace.

Julia Dearden

Theatre includes: The Winter's Tale, The
Crucible (RSC); Dancing at Lughnasa
(Garrick); Camille (Comedy); The Shaughran
(RNT); The Silver Tassie (Almeida); Romeo
and Juliet (ESC); Una Pooka, The Mai
(Tricycle); Pentecost, Into the Heartland, Ruby,
Caught Red Handed (Tinderbox Theatre
Company); Women on the Verge of HRT,
The Laughter of Our Children (Dubbeljoint
Productions); Lengthening Shadows, The
Merchant of Venice, The Importance of Being
Earnest, The Blind Fiddler (Lyric, Belfast).
Television and film includes: The Billy Plays,
Troubles, Cal, The Gravy Train, Fools of
Fortune, Oranges and Lemons, Lost
Belongings, The Nation's Health, Clarissa,
Titanic Town, Wild about Harry.

Ian Dickinson (sound designer)

For the Royal Court: The Sugar Syndrome,
Blood, Playing the Victim, Fallout, Flesh
Wound, Hitchcock Blonde (& Lyric), Black
Milk, Crazyblackmuthafuckin'self, Caryl
Churchill Shorts, Imprint, Mother Teresa is
Dead, Push Up, Workers Writes, Fucking
Games, Herons, Cutting Through the
Carnival.
Other theatre includes: Port (Royal Exchange,
Manchester); Night of the Soul (RSC
Barbican); Eyes of the Kappa (Gate); Crime
and Punishment in Dalston (Arcola Theatre);
Search and Destroy (New End, Hampstead);
Phaedra, Three Sisters, The Shaughraun,
Writer's Cramp (Royal Lyceum, Edinburgh);
The Whore's Dream (RSC Fringe, Edinburgh);
As You Like It, An Experienced Woman Gives
Advice, Present Laughter, The Philadelphia
Story, Wolks World, Poor Superman, Martin
Yesterday, Fast Food, Coyote Ugly, Prizenight
(Royal Exchange, Manchester).
Ian is Head of Sound at the Royal Court.

Michelle Fairley

For the Royal Court: The Weir (& Broadway), Neverland, Oleanna.
Other theatre includes: Scenes from a Big Picture (RNT); Midden (Rough Magic/ Hampstead); Death and the Maiden (The Old Museum Arts Centre, Belfast); Dr Faustus, Philadelphia, Here I Come (Tron, Glasgow); The Hostage, Pentecost, Factory Girls (Tricycle); Joyriders (Paines Plough); Don Juan, Slave Island (Royal Exchange, Manchester); Lady from the Sea (Citizens, Glasgow); By the Border (RNT Studio); The Doctor of Honour (Cheek by Jowl tour); Leonce and Lena (Crucible, Sheffield); The Shadow of a Gunman (Ireland/US tour).
Television includes: The Clinic, Holby City, Inspector Rebus, In Deep, McReady and Daughter, Births, Marriages and Deaths, Vicious Circle, Tom Jones, The Broker's Man, Precious Blood, Safe and Sound, A Mug's Game, Inspector Morse: A Walk through the Woods, Life after Life, Cardiac Arrest, Comics, The Long Roads, Force of Duty, Fleabites, Children of the North, Pentecost, Valentine Falls, Saracens, Hidden City, Cross Fire.
Film includes: The Others, Hideous Kinky, A Soldier's Daughter Never Cries, Hidden Agenda.

Elizabeth Freestone (assistant director)

As assistant director, theatre includes:
Sunday Father (Hampstead); The Trestle at Pope Lick Creek (Southwark Playhouse); Navy Pier (Soho); The Pilgrimage, Macbeth (British Council Far East tour).
As director, theatre includes: Lemon Love (Finborough); Early to Rise, A Different Kind of Dancing (Soho Theatre Studio).
As producer, theatre includes: The Destiny of Me (Finborough).
As producer, radio includes: A Ring Around the Bath, The Change, Who Wears the Trousers?, The Matchmaker (Radio 4).
Elizabeth is also a script reader for Hampstead Theatre, Salisbury Playhouse and the RSC.

Lisa Hogg

Theatre includes: Many Loves (Lillian Bayliss); In the Jungle of the City (Windsor Arts Centre/ Drill Hall); War Crimes Tribunal (Soho); The Wizard of Oz (Ulster Theatre Company); The Fisher King, Women through the Ages, She Stoops to Conquer, Shirley Valentine, War of Words (Lyric, Belfast); Our Town (Millennium Dome/Waterfront Hall, Belfast).
Television includes: Guardian, Brookside.

Sinéad Keenan

Theatre includes: My Fair Lady, West Side Story, The Crucible (Young People's Theatre); A Child's Christmas in Wales (Abbey); Dark Side of the Moon (UCD Dramasoc).
Television includes: Fair City (RTE), The Cassidys (RTE), Murder Squad (ITV).
Film includes: Sunburn, On the Nose, Conspiracy of Silence, Bite.

Cara Kelly

For the Royal Court: On Raftery's Hill (co-production with Druid Theatre Company), The Steward of Christendom (co-production with Out of Joint), King Lear, All Things Nice.
Other theatre includes: Top Girls (Stoke); The Life of Galileo (Almeida); Playboy of the Western World, Therese Raquin (Communicado); You Never Can Tell (West Yorkshire Playhouse); Juno and the Paycock, Ghosts (Royal Lyceum, Edinburgh); Macbeth (Brunton Theatre); Sharp Shorts (Traverse); The Winter's Tale, Miss Julie (Young Vic).
Television includes: Sunday, State of Play, Holy Cross, River City, The Precious Blood, Life Supprt, Between the Lines.
Cara won the Radio 4 Carleton Hobbs Award.

Stephen Kennedy

For the Royal Court: The Force of Change.
Other theatre includes: Popcorn (Liverpool Playhouse); Comedians, The Contractor (Oxford Stage Company); Juno and the Paycock (Donmar); Measure for Measure, Shadows (RSC); This Lime Tree Bower (RSC Fringe); Translations (Royal Lyceum, Edinburgh); Phaedra (Gate, Dublin); Double Helix, On the Outside, Silverlands, The Winter Thief, On the Inside, Away Alone (Peacock, Dublin); Miss Julie (Andrew's Lane); Macbeth (Kilkenny Castle); The Taming of the Shrew (Lyric, Belfast); Belfry (Druid Theatre Company); Hamlet, The Honey Spike (Abbey, Dublin); Donny Boy (Tinderbox Theatre Company).
Television includes: Making Waves, The Vice, On Home Ground, Shockers 11 - Parent's Night, Father Ted, Ballykissangel, The Hanging Gale, The Snapper.
Film includes: Sylvester, Nothing Personal, Braveheart.

Valerie Lilley

For the Royal Court: On Raftery's Hill (co-production with Druid Theatre Company), Blue Heart, Killing the Cat (co-production with Soho Theatre Company), Inventing a New Colour (co-production with Bristol Old Vic), Flying Blind.

Other theatre includes: The True Life & Fiction of Mata Hari (Palace, Watford); The Beauty Queen of Leenane (Salisbury Playhouse); Holy Mothers (Ambassadors); The Mai, A Love Song for Ulster, Factory Girls (Tricycle); Drive On (Lyric, Belfast); Pig's Ear (Liverpool Playhouse Studio); Lysistrata, Juno and the Paycock (Contact, Manchester); My Mother Said I Never Should, Blood Wedding, Some Kind of Hero (Bolton Octagon); Jane Eyre (Sheffield Crucible); The Cherry Orchard, The Card, Once a Catholic (New Victoria, Stoke); Madhouse in Goa (Oldham Coliseum); Soapbox (Library, Manchester); Shadow of a Gunman, Skirmishes, Breezeblock Park, All My Sons (Liverpool Playhouse); On Yer Bike (Belgrade, Coventry); Kennedy's Children, Beggar's Opera, Flying Blind, Camino Real, Coming and Goings (Everyman, Liverpool); John, Paul, George, Ringo and Bert (West End); The Plough and the Stars (Nottingham Playhouse); Ghosts, Hamlet (Victoria, Stoke-on-Trent); Shadow of a Gunman (Mermaid).

Film includes: Cheeky, Priest, Scrubbers. Television includes: Serious and Organised, Grange Hill, Crime & Punishment, Anybody's Nightmare, First Communion Day, Hope and Glory, Peak Practice, The Rag Nymph, Famous Five, Brookside, Missing Persons, Elidor, Blood on the Dole, The Riff Raff Element, EastEnders, Nice Town, Children of the North, The Bill, Loving Hazel, Minder, The Refuge, Final Run, Albion Market, Night of a Campaign, Give us a Break, The Long March, Scully, Coronation Street.

Mark McCrory

Theatre includes: As the Beast Sleeps (Tricycle); Sinking (Irish tour); Besieged (Millennium Forum); Henry Joy McCracken (Irish tour). Film and television includes: H3 The Movie, Deadlands, Gun, Titanic Town, The Comedies of Eire.

Christopher Oram (designer)

For the Royal Court: Fucking Games. Other theatre includes: The Marriage Play/ Finding the Sun, Summerfolk (RNT); Don Juan, Edward II, As You Like It, Six Degrees of Separation, Twelfth Night, What the Butler Saw (Sheffield Crucible); Merrily We Roll Along, Passion Play, Good, The Bullet (Donmar); Dinner With Friends (Hampstead); The Jew of Malta, The Doctor's Dilemma (Almeida); A Life (Abbey, Dublin); Aristocrats (Gate, Dublin); A Streetcar Named Desire, All My Sons (Bristol Old Vic).

David Plater (lighting designer)

Theatre includes: My Night with Reg (New Victoria, Stoke); Moment of Weakness (Belgrade, Coventry & national tour); A Passionate Woman, When We are Married (Theatre Royal, York); The Double Bass, Blackbird, Trip's Cinch, Mongoose, Eskimo Sisters (Southwark Playhouse); Amy's View (Theatre Royal, Windsor/Yvonne Arnaud, Guildford); Frame 312, Three Days of Rain, Morphic Resonance, Splash Hatch, Summer Begins, Bad Finger, The Other Side of the Rainbow (Donmar); What You Get and What You Expect (Lyric, Hammersmith); What Now Little Man (Greenwich); Dark Tales (Arts); The Dave Strassmen Show (Apollo); Love on the Dole (Oldham Coliseum/Theatre Royal, Hanley & national tour); The Relationship, Island Sea, Falling Through (Riverside); Girls Were Made to Love and Kiss (Old Fire Station, Oxford); Oliver (National Youth Music Theatre); Count Ory (New Sussex Opera); One Last Surviving, Entertaining Strangers, Dark Side of the Moon (Lyric Studio, Hammersmith); Cherry Orchard (Horsham); The Nun, Out in the Cold, The Green Parakeet, Erasmus Montanus, A Spanner in the Works, And Woman Must Weep, The Will (Greenwich Studio).

Josie Rourke (director)

For the Royal Court, as director: Crazyblackmuthafuckin'self and Children's Day. For the Royal Court and English Touring Theatre, as assistant director: The York Realist. As an assistant director she has worked for Michael Grandage, Nicholas Hytner, Phyllida Lloyd and Sam Mendes (Donmar Warehouse) and Peter Gill (Royal National Theatre). As director, other theatre includes: World Music (Sheffield Crucible); Romeo & Juliet (Liverpool Playhouse); Kick for Touch (Sheffield Theatre); Frame 312 (Donmar). Future projects include: My Dad's A Birdman (Young Vic); World Music (Donmar). Josie is a Trainee Associate Director at the Royal Court.

THE ENGLISH STAGE COMPANY AT THE ROYAL COURT

The English Stage Company at the Royal Court opened in 1956 as a subsidised theatre producing new British plays, international plays and some classical revivals.

The first artistic director George Devine aimed to create a writers' theatre, 'a place where the dramatist is acknowledged as the fundamental creative force in the theatre and where the play is more important than the actors, the director, the designer'. The urgent need was to find a contemporary style in which the play, the acting, direction and design are all combined. He believed that 'the battle will be a long one to continue to create the right conditions for writers to work in'.

Devine aimed to discover 'hard-hitting, uncompromising writers whose plays are stimulating, provocative and exciting'. The Royal Court production of John Osborne's Look Back in Anger in May 1956 is now seen as the decisive starting point of modern British drama and the policy created a new generation of British playwrights. The first wave included John Osborne, Arnold Wesker, John Arden, Ann Jellicoe, N F Simpson and Edward Bond. Early seasons included new international plays by Bertolt Brecht, Eugène Ionesco, Samuel Beckett, Jean-Paul Sartre and Marguerite Duras.

The theatre started with the 400-seat proscenium arch Theatre Downstairs, and then in 1969 opened a second theatre, the 60-seat studio Theatre Upstairs. Some productions transfer to the West End, such as Terry Johnson's Hitchcock Blonde, Caryl Churchill's Far Away, Conor McPherson's The Weir, Kevin Elyot's Mouth to Mouth and My Night With Reg. The Royal Court also co-produces plays which have transferred to the West End or toured internationally, such as Sebastian Barry's The Steward of Christendom and Mark Ravenhill's Shopping and Fucking (with Out of Joint), Martin McDonagh's The Beauty Queen Of Leenane (with Druid Theatre Company), Ayub Khan-Din's East is East (with Tamasha Theatre Company, and now a feature film).

Since 1994 the Royal Court's artistic policy has again been vigorously directed to finding and producing a new generation of playwrights. The writers include Joe Penhall, Rebecca Prichard, Michael Wynne, Nick Grosso, Judy Upton, Meredith Oakes, Sarah Kane, Anthony Neilson, Judith Johnson, James Stock, Jez Butterworth, Marina Carr, Phyllis Nagy, Simon Block, Martin McDonagh, Mark Ravenhill, Ayub Khan-Din, Tamantha Hammerschlag, Jess Walters, Ché Walker, Conor McPherson, Simon Stephens,

photo: Andy Chopping

Richard Bean, Roy Williams, Gary Mitchell, Mick Mahoney, Rebecca Gilman, Christopher Shinn, Kia Corthron, David Gieselmann, Marius von Mayenburg, David Eldridge, Leo Butler, Zinnie Harris, Grae Cleugh, Roland Schimmelpfennig, DeObia Oparei, Vassily Sigarev, the Presnyakov Brothers and Lucy Prebble. This expanded programme of new plays has been made possible through the support of A.S.K Theater Projects and the Skirball Foundation, the Jerwood Charitable Foundation, the American Friends of the Royal Court Theatre and many in association with the Royal National Theatre Studio.

In recent years there have been record-breaking productions at the box office, with capacity houses for Roy Williams' Fallout, Terry Johnson's Hitchcock Blonde, Caryl Churchill's A Number, Jez Butterworth's The Night Heron, Rebecca Gilman's Boy Gets Girl, Kevin Elyot's Mouth to Mouth, David Hare's My Zinc Bed and Conor McPherson's The Weir, which transferred to the West End in October 1998 and ran for nearly two years at the Duke of York's Theatre.

The newly refurbished theatre in Sloane Square opened in February 2000, with a policy still inspired by the first artistic director George Devine. The Royal Court is an international theatre for new plays and new playwrights, and the work shapes contemporary drama in Britain and overseas.

AWARDS FOR
THE ROYAL COURT

Jez Butterworth won the 1995 George Devine Award, the Writers' Guild New Writer of the Year Award, the Evening Standard Award for Most Promising Playwright and the Olivier Award for Best Comedy for Mojo.

The Royal Court was the overall winner of the 1995 Prudential Award for the Arts for creativity, excellence, innovation and accessibility. The Royal Court Theatre Upstairs won the 1995 Peter Brook Empty Space Award for innovation and excellence in theatre.

Michael Wynne won the 1996 Meyer-Whitworth Award for The Knocky. Martin McDonagh won the 1996 George Devine Award, the 1996 Writers' Guild Best Fringe Play Award, the 1996 Critics' Circle Award and the 1996 Evening Standard Award for Most Promising Playwright for The Beauty Queen of Leenane. Marina Carr won the 19th Susan Smith Blackburn Prize (1996/7) for Portia Coughlan. Conor McPherson won the 1997 George Devine Award, the 1997 Critics' Circle Award and the 1997 Evening Standard Award for Most Promising Playwright for The Weir. Ayub Khan-Din won the 1997 Writers' Guild Awards for Best West End Play and Writers' Guild New Writer of the Year and the 1996 John Whiting Award for East is East (co-production with Tamasha).

At the 1998 Tony Awards, Martin McDonagh's The Beauty Queen of Leenane (co-production with Druid Theatre Company) won four awards including Garry Hynes for Best Director and was nominated for a further two. Eugene Ionesco's The Chairs (co-production with Theatre de Complicite) was nominated for six Tony awards. David Hare won the 1998 Time Out Live Award for Outstanding Achievement and six awards in New York including the Drama League, Drama Desk and New York Critics Circle Award for Via Dolorosa. Sarah Kane won the 1998 Arts Foundation Fellowship in Playwriting. Rebecca Prichard won the 1998 Critics' Circle Award for Most Promising Playwright for Yard Gal (co-production with Clean Break).

Conor McPherson won the 1999 Olivier Award for Best New Play for The Weir. The Royal Court won the 1999 ITI Award for Excellence in International Theatre. Sarah Kane's Cleansed was judged Best Foreign Language Play in 1999 by Theater Heute in Germany. Gary Mitchell won the 1999 Pearson Best Play Award for Trust. Rebecca Gilman was joint winner of the 1999 George Devine Award and won the 1999 Evening Standard Award for Most Promising Playwright for The Glory of Living.

In 1999, the Royal Court won the European theatre prize New Theatrical Realities, presented at Taormina Arte in Sicily, for its efforts in recent years in discovering and producing the work of young British dramatists.

Roy Williams and Gary Mitchell were joint winners of the George Devine Award 2000 for Most Promising Playwright for Lift Off and The Force of Change respectively. At the Barclays Theatre Awards 2000 presented by the TMA, Richard Wilson won the Best Director Award for David Gieselmann's Mr Kolpert and Jeremy Herbert won the Best Designer Award for Sarah Kane's 4.48 Psychosis. Gary Mitchell won the Evening Standard's Charles Wintour Award 2000 for Most Promising Playwright for The Force of Change. Stephen Jeffreys' I Just Stopped by to See The Man won an AT&T: On Stage Award 2000.

David Eldridge's Under the Blue Sky won the Time Out Live Award 2001 for Best New Play in the West End. Leo Butler won the George Devine Award 2001 for Most Promising Playwright for Redundant. Roy Williams won the Evening Standard's Charles Wintour Award 2001 for Most Promising Playwright for Clubland. Grae Cleugh won the 2001 Olivier Award for Most Promising Playwright for Fucking Games. Richard Bean was joint winner of the George Devine Award 2002 for Most Promising Playwright for Under the Whaleback. Caryl Churchill won the 2002 Evening Standard Award for Best New Play for A Number. Vassily Sigarev won the 2002 Evening Standard Charles Wintour Award for Most Promising Playwright for Plasticine. Ian MacNeil won the 2002 Evening Standard Award for Best Design for A Number and Plasticine. Peter Gill won the 2002 Critics' Circle Award for Best New Play for The York Realist (English Touring Theatre). Ché Walker won the 2003 George Devine Award for Most Promising Playwright for Flesh Wound.

ROYAL COURT BOOKSHOP

The bookshop offers a wide range of playtexts and theatre books, with over 1,000 titles. Located in the downstairs Bar and Food area, the bookshop is open Monday to Saturday, afternoons and evenings.

Many Royal Court playtexts are available for just £2 including works by Harold Pinter, Caryl Churchill, Rebecca Gilman, Martin Crimp, Sarah Kane, Conor McPherson, Ayub Khan-Din, Timberlake Wertenbaker and Roy Williams.

For information on titles and special events, Email: bookshop@royalcourttheatre.com
Tel: 020 7565 5024

PROGRAMME SUPPORTERS

The Royal Court (English Stage Company Ltd) receives its principal funding from London Arts. It is also supported financially by a wide range of private companies and public bodies and earns the remainder of its income from the box office and its own trading activities.
The Royal Borough of Kensington & Chelsea gives an annual grant to the Royal Court Young Writers' Programme.

The Jerwood Charitable Foundation continues to support new plays by new playwrights through the Jerwood New Playwrights series. Since 1993 A.S.K. Theater Projects and the Skirball Foundation have funded a Playwrights' Programme at the theatre. Bloomberg Mondays, the Royal Court's reduced price ticket scheme, is supported by Bloomberg. Over the past seven years the BBC has supported the Gerald Chapman Fund for directors.

ROYAL COURT
AUTUMN 2003

JERWOOD THEATRE UPSTAIRS

Until 15 November
THE SUGAR SYNDROME
by **Lucy Prebble**
Directed by Marianne Elliott

Cast: Will Ash, Kate Duchene, Stephanie Leonidas, Andrew Woodall.

Design: Jonathan Fensom, Lighting Design: Chris Davey, Sound Design: Ian Dickinson.

Dani's on a mission. She's 17, hates her parents, skives college and prefers life in the chatroom on-line. What she's looking for is someone who is honest and direct. What she finds is a man twice her age who thinks she's an 11-year-old boy.

Supported by
the Royal Court's PRODUCTION SYNDICATE scheme

26 November - 10 January
A Royal Court and Out of Joint co-production
DUCK by **Stella Feehily**
Directed by Max Stafford-Clark

Cast: Gina Moxley, Ruth Negga, Aidan O'Hare, Tony Rohr, Karl Shiels, Elaine Symons.

Design: Jonathan Fensom, Lighting Design Johanna Town, Sound Design: Paul Arditti.

Cat's got big feet so her boyfriend calls her Duck. She's also got a middle-aged lover, a boyfriend with a gun, and a brainy best friend with a short fuse. They're teenagers on the brink, growing up in the face of everything a city can throw at them But girls just wanna have fun. Can you learn to be good when your elders are no longer your betters? Somehow, the girls must cope - or find a way of escaping.

BOX OFFICE 020 7565 5000
www.royalcourttheatre.com

London Government · ARTS COUNCIL ENGLAND

LOYAL WOMEN

Gary Mitchell

Love to Alison

Characters

The Fords:

BRENDA FORD, *thirty-three*

JENNY, *Brenda's daughter, sixteen*

RITA, *Brenda's mother-in-law, fifty-eight*

TERRY, *Brenda's husband, thirty-four*

BABY, *Brenda's granddaughter, six months*

Women's Local UDA

MAUREEN, *Branch Head, fifty-four*

GAIL, *Second in Command, thirty*

HEATHER, *active Women's UDA operative, thirty-two*

Other characters

ADELE, *the accused, nineteen*

MARK, *Brenda's friend, thirty-one*

Location: the Ford family home. Living room and parlour converted into temporary bedroom.

Scene One

BRENDA *is in the parlour with* RITA. *The parlour has been converted temporarily into a bedroom for* RITA *complete with commode.* JENNY *is in the living room watching TV. The living room is in a state of disarray.* MARK *is putting the finishing touches to a brick fireplace and continually journeys from his workplace to the back garden where he keeps the bricks, sand etc.* BRENDA *is washing* RITA. *A Christmas tree is lying at the side of the fireplace waiting to be assembled and decorated.*

BRENDA (*calling into living room*). Jenny, can you come and get this please?

RITA. Your man's coming back into Coronation Street tonight.

BRENDA. Jenny? (*To* RITA.) I think there's a match on, Rita.

MARK *watches* JENNY *aware that she is being called and ignoring her mother.*

RITA. Terry can watch the football in the living room and you can watch Coronation Street in here with me.

BRENDA. The football's on instead. You'll have to wait until after.

RITA. Well then we can all watch the football with Terry in the living room.

BRENDA. Jenny? Can you come in here please?

RITA. I'll give you some money and you can get something for a wee cup of tea.

MARK. Will I go and see what she wants?

BRENDA. Jenny?

RITA. Get those wee chocolate buns that Terry loves.

JENNY *moves to the door connecting the living room to the parlour.*

JENNY. What?

BRENDA. Did you not hear me calling you?

JENNY. The TV must've been too loud.

BRENDA (*indicating commode*). Can you empty this for me?

JENNY. I'm not emptying that.

BRENDA. Just do it love.

JENNY. I can't. It makes me sick.

BRENDA. Do it!

RITA. She wouldn't talk like that if her father was in.

BRENDA. Jenny, you've done nothing all day.

JENNY. How have I not?

BRENDA. Tell me what you've done.

JENNY. Everything.

RITA. I'll tell her father when he comes in that door. He won't be long wiping the smile off her face.

JENNY. How will he when he's not allowed to come here anymore?

RITA. Not allowed to come here?

JENNY. My mum threw him out.

RITA. Does she think we're all crazy?

BRENDA. He is allowed to come here.

RITA. I'll tell him what you said as soon as he sets foot inside this house.

BRENDA. Jenny, just go back to the living room and do whatever you're doing.

JENNY. It's her memory. She remembers nothing.

RITA. I remember respect. In the old days no one would talk like you talk. Does she forget that Christmas presents can be taken back to the shops?

JENNY. I'm really going to be worried about that.

RITA. What? What does she say?

JENNY. What does she ever get me? Socks and hankies.

RITA. Socks and hankies?

JENNY. I don't mind helping Mummy, but I just can't do that.

BRENDA. That's all I need done.

> JENNY *returns to the living room and as* RITA *continues to talk she turns the volume of the TV up.* BABY *cries can be heard through the monitor.*

RITA. If a young person had spoken like that they would've got smacked in the legs or worse. A smack does you no harm. You should think about that. It's not right. No respect. I might be old but I'm not daft.

BRENDA. Don't upset yourself.

> RITA *begins to sob.* BRENDA *feels sorry for her and gives her a hug.*

RITA. In my day you would've been glad of socks and hankies. I never had a hanky until I got one for Christmas and sure you always need a hanky.

BRENDA. You got her perfume.

RITA. So what is she on about?

> BRENDA *stands and leaves the flannel in the basin at* RITA's *feet.*

BRENDA. Can you do your own bits while I empty this?

> BRENDA *takes the basin from the commode to empty it in the kitchen.* RITA *motions to wash herself but is clearly too tired and so gets into bed.* BRENDA *returns.*

I'll wash your hair in the morning, OK?

RITA *puts her TV on and flicks through the channels.*

RITA. Where's Coronation Street? I can't work this thing.

BRENDA. It's on later. Read your book and I'll let you know when it comes on. (*To living room.*) Jenny, turn that down your granny's going to read.

JENNY *doesn't turn it down.*

MARK. Turn it down or Santa won't leave you anything good.

JENNY. You're hilarious.

BRENDA *positions the pillows for* RITA *to sit up comfortably and hands her a book.* RITA *reads.*

BRENDA. Do you want your own light on?

RITA. Don't fuss. You go out and have a nice time with Terry.

BRENDA *goes into the living room.* BABY *can be heard crying through the baby monitor.*

BRENDA. Jenny, will you go and see if she's all right?

JENNY *gets up annoyed and makes her way to the stairs that lead to the bedrooms.* BRENDA *sits and automatically turns the TV off.*

MARK. I'm going to knock off early and go home and get ready for tonight. You're not going to stand me up again are you?

BRENDA. I don't mean to.

MARK *is gutted.*

What about this weekend? I promise I'll make it up to you.

MARK. No pressure. I understand.

BRENDA. I'm exhausted and I wouldn't be good company.

MARK. You're always good company, Brenda.

BRENDA. This weekend we'll go into town, somewhere nice.

MARK. What about dinner?

BRENDA. Sure I've to make everybody's dinner, it would be easier to make you something with us.

MARK. Fair enough. Have you heard anything from Terry?

BRENDA. He says he's staying with somebody for a couple of days.

MARK. Do you know who?

BRENDA. I've a good idea. Heather.

MARK. How do you feel about that?

BRENDA. She's welcome to him as far as I'm concerned. Once a man is unfaithful to his wife that's him finished. I don't care how much Terry goes on about it being only one night or how many times he promises it will never happen again. He might as well be dead as far as I'm concerned.

MARK. Have you said anything to her? I mean you live in the same street. Have you bumped into her since?

BRENDA. I see her every day. If she's not here with Gail she's borrowing a cup of sugar or some smokes.

MARK. That must be awkward.

BRENDA. It's not her fault. I saw her at Terry's big welcome home from prison party and she was so drunk it could've been any man that went with her. But it wasn't any man. It was Terry and he knew what he was doing.

JENNY *returns.*

Are you still on schedule to finish before Christmas Day?

MARK. Of course I am.

MARK *goes back to work.*

JENNY. Can you go up and see what's wrong. She won't stop crying.

BRENDA. Did you try lifting her?

JENNY. She's heavy.

BRENDA *rushes out of the room.*

Who put the TV off?

MARK. Your mum – she wanted a bit of quiet.

JENNY. Maybe Santa will bring her some.

MARK. Keep it low at least.

> JENNY *puts the TV on, turning the volume up as it comes on and slouches on the settee engrossed.* MARK *watches her.* RITA *calls from her room.*

RITA. Brenda? Brenda, can you come in here please?

> MARK *waits to see if* JENNY *is going to move.* JENNY *remains oblivious to* RITA. MARK *goes into* RITA's *room.*

MARK. Do you need something love?

RITA. Brenda, there's a man in my room. What are you doing here?

MARK. It's me, Mark.

RITA. Stay where you are. (*Shouts.*) Brenda!

MARK. What do you need?

RITA. Get out of my bedroom. My son Terry will be home from work soon. He's a very big man – top man in the UDA just got out of jail – he'll soon show you the door.

> BRENDA *rushes through the living room with* BABY *in her arms.* MARK *backs out as* BRENDA *enters the room.*

There's a man in my room, did you not hear me calling you?

BRENDA. It's only Mark.

RITA. You shouldn't have strange men in the house when Terry's not here it's inappropriate.

BRENDA. What do you want?

RITA. I want Terry.

BRENDA. We've talked about this.

RITA. Well as soon as he sets foot in here let him know I want to talk to him.

BRENDA. Is that it?

RITA. Let me see her.

BRENDA. I'll hold her for you.

RITA. She's gorgeous. I told you Terry wanted another little girl. He's great with children and one child isn't a family.

The telephone rings and BRENDA *is up and away.* JENNY *picks up the telephone before* BRENDA *gets there.*

JENNY. No, it's me, Gail? Do you want her?

BRENDA *takes the telephone and offers* BABY *to* JENNY *who turns away and watches TV.*

BRENDA. Sorry, what? I can't hear you.

BRENDA *indicates that* JENNY *should turn the TV off and compromises with lowering the volume.*

Tonight? I can't make it tonight.

BRENDA *listens and hushes* BABY. MARK *stops work.*

I'm having work done and the place is a mess, where would everybody sit? No, honestly, not tonight. (*Listens and becomes distressed.*) Eight?

BRENDA *struggles to put the telephone back.*

JENNY. What is it?

BRENDA. They're having a meeting here tonight.

JENNY. Brilliant, what time at?

BRENDA. It's not brilliant.

JENNY. Who's all coming?

BRENDA. Never mind, you'll be upstairs minding this wee one.

JENNY. No way. I'm not missing this. They said I could join this month – that's probably why they want to hold it here.

BRENDA. Not everything in the world revolves around you, Jenny love.

JENNY. It's perfect. I better get ready.

BRENDA. No, it's not perfect and the only thing you need to get ready is this one. I'm serious Jenny. You get yourself upstairs and sort her out.

JENNY. This is really important.

BRENDA. More important than her?

JENNY. You can put her to sleep and then come down. We've got the monitor and all. You said you were thinking of leaving anyway. So why don't you leave and let me take your place?

BRENDA. It doesn't work like that.

JENNY. I'll talk to them and explain that you have to mind the baby.

BRENDA. No, you have to.

JENNY. Why do I always have to do everything?

BRENDA. That's life.

JENNY. It's shit, my life is always like this.

BRENDA. Always like what?

JENNY. Like this! Whenever something has to be done – it's always me that ends up doing it. She cries all day, I can't stop her. She never goes to sleep when you want her to and I can't do anything that I have to do. I have no life.

BRENDA. Well you should have thought about that before you opened your legs to the first bloke that looked at you.

JENNY *bursts out crying and runs out of the room, leaving* BRENDA *holding* BABY.

JENNY. I'm telling my daddy what you said.

MARK. Could you not have told them to make it some other night?

BRENDA. It was Gail and you know what she's like – you can't tell Gail anything.

MARK. What do you want me to do about this?

BRENDA. You'll have to stop and come back again tomorrow.

MARK *checks his watch.* BRENDA *puts* BABY *in her pram as* MARK *takes everything out to the back garden.* BRENDA *then begins to tidy the place as best she can. When* MARK *returns* BRENDA *is still busy tidying.* MARK *begins to help and* BRENDA *stops him.*

You should go before they get here.

BRENDA *kisses* MARK *on the cheek.*

I'm sorry.

MARK *attempts to kiss her back but she is too quick and returns to her tidying.* MARK *waits for a second and then gathers his gear and leaves.*

Scene Two

RITA *is in bed smoking and watching television.* BRENDA
comes downstairs. RITA *stubs out her cigarette and hides the
evidence of smoke.* BRENDA *and* MAUREEN *enter the living
room.* MAUREEN *takes her coat off – she is wearing a suit.*
BRENDA *looks in on* RITA *and then returns her attention to
the living room.* GAIL *and* HEATHER *enter and* JENNY
closes the door. GAIL *is wearing all denim and boots.*
HEATHER *is wearing a jogging suit and trainers. When*
JENNY *enters the living room* MAUREEN *hands her the
coats.*

MAUREEN. Put these on a bed upstairs please.

> JENNY *shrugs and lethargically walks out of the room.*
> MAUREEN *closes the door, shutting* JENNY *out from the
> meeting.*

Brenda, Heather, before we start. Any personal problems
you two might have with each other you can sort out after
this meeting. This is WUDA business only. Do we
understand each other?

HEATHER. I've already said what happened. Somebody
spiked my drink, you know me Brenda – I'm not like that.

GAIL. When a person hasn't had sex for sixteen years they'll
do anything for a bit.

BRENDA. I don't care how long he hasn't had sex for what he
did was unforgivable.

GAIL. I was talking about Heather.

MAUREEN. Does Jenny know?

BRENDA. No. And there won't be any problems with me and
Heather.

MAUREEN. Good.

HEATHER *checks to see if everyone believes this. They take their seats.*

BRENDA. Do you want a wee cup of tea before you start?

GAIL. Do the tea later, Brenda. Business first.

HEATHER. I'd love a wee cup of tea.

GAIL. What did I just say?

JENNY *opens the door, talking on her mobile telephone.*

BRENDA. Even just tea to heat you up? You look freezing.

GAIL. Put the heating on.

MAUREEN. Close the doors and we'll be fine.

BRENDA. Jenny, close that door.

JENNY *comes into the living room.*

JENNY. Love ya, bye.

JENNY *puts her mobile phone in her pocket.*

BRENDA. I meant from the outside we're having a meeting here.

GAIL. Let her stay if she behaves.

MAUREEN. It might not do the young ones a bit of harm to listen in.

BRENDA. I don't want her involved in anything like this.

HEATHER. You make it sound like a bad thing, Brenda.

BRENDA. I thought it was private.

HEATHER (*to* JENNY). Sit down and button it wee girl. One word and I'll knock you out.

GAIL. One word and you are out.

MAUREEN. Let's open with a prayer please. Heather?

HEATHER (*to* JENNY). Eyes closed.

They bow their heads and close their eyes.

Thank you, lord for keeping our friends and family and loved ones safe. Thank you, lord for forgiving us our sins too. Thank you, lord for your son Jesus Christ, Amen.

GAIL. Amen!

JENNY *and* BRENDA. Amen!

MAUREEN. Amen. I now declare D Company, Rathcoole District weekly meeting open. Gail – first order of business please.

GAIL. First order of business is we need to appoint a new district treasurer.

HEATHER. I nominate me.

GAIL. You can't nominate yourself.

HEATHER. How do you get nominated then?

MAUREEN. Like this. I nominate Brenda.

HEATHER. Can I second it? Wait I'm not Brenda. Nominate me.

BRENDA. Let her do it.

MAUREEN. Do I hear a second?

JENNY. Can I second it?

BRENDA. You're not a member.

HEATHER. That's right, you have to be a member.

GAIL. I second it.

MAUREEN. Good. Brenda, you're now treasurer of Rathcoole Women's Ulster Defence Association. Congratulations.

BRENDA. I'm really too busy.

MAUREEN. A lot of people put their names forward for this Brenda.

GAIL. It's a great opportunity.

HEATHER. That's why I wanted to do it.

JENNY. Mummy, it's brilliant.

BRENDA. Honestly, I've too much on my plate at the minute.

MAUREEN. You will be given the books and all dues and donations will be delivered to you here and all you do is note them and make a list of all members who do not pay and present that list to me on Friday night at the club.

GAIL. It's an afternoon's work.

BRENDA. It's a lot of responsibility.

MAUREEN. Why do you think we're offering this to you, Brenda? Why not give it to one of the many applicants and there were many? Because people who offer to be treasurer of anything are thinking about one thing and one thing only.

GAIL. Getting their grubby little hands on our money.

HEATHER. You're not saying that about me, are you?

MAUREEN. Fiddling books. Creaming a little off the top.

HEATHER. I would stop that happening.

GAIL. This brings me handily enough to the second point of business. What are we going to do with Mrs Watson?

BRENDA. We haven't finished the first one yet.

GAIL. We have.

JENNY. But my mummy hasn't accepted yet, she means.

MAUREEN. Your appointment has been noted and I will report it to the county leaders by telephone and it will be included in our newsletter by the end of the week. Second point of business Gail.

GAIL. Mrs Watson. Fees, funds, donations, dues have all been getting less and less for the past six months. Now, either we're losing support in the community or Mrs Watson has been misplacing the money.

HEATHER. I say we do her.

BRENDA. Mrs Watson is an old lady, Maureen and she's been doing the books for years.

GAIL. What's your point?

BRENDA. Why would she start ripping us off now?

JENNY. Is that Mrs Watson from Carnreagh Bend?

MAUREEN. The very one.

JENNY. Guilty. She is stealing money Mummy. She must be 'cause they just got a new car.

BRENDA. That's her husband's and he got it with his disability living allowance. Every person who gets sick now gets a free car you know that.

HEATHER. I say we do her anyway just in case.

BRENDA. I'll take this job if you leave her alone. Let her retire…gently.

HEATHER. Let her get away with it you mean.

GAIL. It hasn't been proven, she is old and maybe we should be looking over those books to see who really was paying.

MAUREEN. Maybe Brenda could have a wee talk with her and see if she can find out who was paying and who wasn't paying.

HEATHER. And then we could do them.

GAIL. Then we could speak to them.

HEATHER. And then do them.

JENNY *laughs, she loves this sort of talk.*

MAUREEN. Do you think you could talk to her, Brenda?

BRENDA. I'll try.

GAIL. She probably got too old and frail to tell on people.

JENNY. She's only a wee woman like. What could she do if somebody threatened her?

MAUREEN. I'm sure Brenda will know who is paying and who isn't after a couple of weeks.

GAIL. And if anybody tries it on with you Brenda what would you do?

BRENDA. It depends.

HEATHER. You tell us.

BRENDA. If I'm going to do this for you, Maureen, I'll do it my own way.

GAIL. What way would that be?

BRENDA. Give people some time to pay. Maybe not collect any money at Christmas and other times like this when money is tight for everybody.

MAUREEN. I like that. Build up a good rapport.

BRENDA. Let people know that we're easing the burden at difficult times. And listen and find out why somebody can't pay or doesn't want to pay or whatever and then maybe give them a little time.

GAIL. Can't be too lenient with some people Brenda.

BRENDA. We can't force people to pay.

HEATHER. Can we not?

BRENDA. It is voluntary. If it's not you can count me out.

GAIL. It is voluntary but I just want to know who is paying and who isn't paying and why they aren't paying.

MAUREEN. It's all for information just.

GAIL. We wouldn't want people claiming to be fully supportive and benefiting from all the WUDA have to offer if they weren't paying their dues now would we?

MAUREEN. Third point of business.

GAIL. We received information two weeks ago about two catholic men coming into Rathcoole on a regular basis.

JENNY. I know about this.

MAUREEN *gestures* JENNY *should be quiet.*

GAIL. These two men were of course warned about coming in to the estate and that seems to have been enough for one of them but the oldest one is persistent and has continued to return.

JENNY. He's going with Adele White.

GAIL. Correct.

BRENDA. If the men can't keep him out of the estate what can we do?

GAIL. They want us to have a chat with Adele. (*To* HEATHER.) Don't say it.

HEATHER. I wasn't going to say anything.

JENNY. I know what she was going to say.

MAUREEN. Brenda what would you think of having a wee chat with her here?

GAIL. She knows us, so we can't ask her or she might think we're threatening her.

MAUREEN. And we don't want to do that yet.

BRENDA. I'm already doing the treasurer thing for you isn't that enough?

MAUREEN. Of course it is. I'm just asking – because I know what you're like.

BRENDA. What am I like?

MAUREEN. Let me put it this way. If Heather here has to talk to her about letting a catholic man into the estate to see her, what way do you think that would go?

JENNY *gestures that* HEATHER *would beat the girl up.* HEATHER *agrees.*

There is no one else Brenda.

HEATHER. We're not asking you to do her.

JENNY. I could go round and see her in her house, she would let me in – she knows me from school. Gail and Heather could wait outside and I could go in and tell her that she's not allowed to see this fenian anymore and if she slabbers or anything like that I could signal to Gail.

BRENDA. I'll talk to her.

GAIL. You have to talk to her tomorrow, Brenda.

MAUREEN. We don't want this guy ruining everybody's Christmas.

HEATHER. Now what about that cup of tea you promised me?

BRENDA *gets up slowly and makes her way to the kitchen.* GAIL *nods at* JENNY *and* JENNY *understands, gets up and follows her mother.*

MAUREEN. What do you think?

GAIL. I think she'll do it.

MAUREEN. If not?

GAIL. Then she's going to have one really shit Christmas.

MAUREEN. Heather, go to the loo.

HEATHER. I don't need to go to the loo. I haven't done anything. Is it about nominating myself?

MAUREEN. No, just go to the loo or answer the door, do something outside of this room.

GAIL *waits for* HEATHER *to leave, she is concerned.*

My retirement party on Saturday is cancelled.

GAIL. That's supposed to be a surprise.

MAUREEN. I have to see this through first.

GAIL. I can see this through.

MAUREEN. I know you can but some people don't.

GAIL. Who like?

MAUREEN. There was a vote at county level and it was decided that maybe, and I stress the 'maybe'.

GAIL. Maybe what?

MAUREEN. Maybe you're not ready yet. Yet!

GAIL. Are you going to give me names?

MAUREEN. Would you do something if I did?

GAIL. No.

MAUREEN. Then you don't need the names.

GAIL. I want to know who's on my side.

MAUREEN. It's only for a couple of weeks and then…everyone will be on your side.

GAIL. You said you would sort this. I hope you're not having second thoughts.

MAUREEN. I'm not having second thoughts.

GAIL. I want assurances that there's no one else in the picture. That it's only me.

MAUREEN. Can you think of anyone else who could do what I do?

GAIL *thinks about this.* GAIL *looks at the door that* BRENDA *went through.*

Scene Three

Banging on front door wakes BABY. BABY *cries.* BRENDA
walks into the living room in her dressing gown, carrying
BABY. TERRY *enters the living room.*

BRENDA. How much do you need?

TERRY. I just want to talk to you love.

BRENDA. You only come here when you want something now
tell me what it is.

TERRY. That's terrible.

BRENDA. That's life.

TERRY. What turned you out like this? What happened to
you?

BRENDA. You. That's what happened to me.

TERRY *practically collapses into a seat.* BRENDA *is
irritated but can't help feel a little sympathy for the man she
once loved.*

TERRY. I used to look forward to meeting up with you and the
main reason was – I know what you're thinking – I loved
that as well like but that wasn't the main thing do you know
what was? You always had that big smile. You were always
happy and I thought – I always want to be with happy
people – they make me happy – just like scumbags make
me not happy.

BRENDA. I'll get you a cup of tea and then you have to hit the
road Terry.

TERRY*'s heart glimpses sadness.* BRENDA *makes her way
to the kitchen.* RITA *wakes.* TERRY *turns the TV on to
escape the thoughts that are making him sad.*

RITA. No cereal for me I like eggs.

BRENDA. It's still nighttime, Rita love, sorry, I'm just going to put the kettle on.

RITA. It's not night it's morning and I want some eggs.

BRENDA *returns from the kitchen with* BABY *in her arms and begins to hush her.*

Don't you hush me I'm not a baby.

BRENDA. I'm making her up a bottle.

BRENDA *walks back into the living room and turns the TV off.*

TERRY. I was watching that.

BRENDA. Make yourself useful.

BRENDA *hands* BABY *to* TERRY. TERRY *body swerves the baby and reaches for the pram.*

TERRY. Put her in here.

BRENDA *keeps* BABY.

BRENDA. You're useless.

RITA. Who is that you're talking to?

TERRY *signals to* BRENDA *that he doesn't want her to say that he is here.*

BRENDA. Nobody.

RITA. I can hear you talking.

BRENDA *goes into the bedroom to show* RITA *the* BABY. TERRY *starts to search the living room.*

BRENDA. I'm talking to the baby trying to make her go to sleep.

RITA. I would like some toast with my eggs please.

BRENDA. It's not morning yet. I will wake you up as soon as it is morning.

RITA. With eggs?

BRENDA. With whatever you want.

TERRY *finds some money and pockets it.*

RITA. Brenda, leave the baby in with me and you go back up and see to Terry.

BRENDA. As much as I'd like to see to him right now I can't.

BRENDA *tucks* RITA *back into bed and returns to the living room.* TERRY *is standing at the door.*

You're up to something.

TERRY. I'm not up to anything.

BRENDA. Why are you standing at the door?

TERRY. I don't want to wake her up.

BRENDA. Then you shouldn't come here in the middle of the night.

TERRY. Get me a key cut and I won't have to wake anybody up ever again.

BRENDA. You don't live here Terry. You're not getting a key.

TERRY. It's my house too, Brenda.

BRENDA. Don't start...how much do you need?

TERRY. Don't be like that. Sit with me for a minute.

BRENDA. I'm too tired. Just tell me how much.

JENNY *comes into the living room.*

JENNY. What's he doing here?

TERRY. Keep your voice down.

JENNY. You can't tell me what to do.

TERRY. You're going to wake my ma up.

BRENDA. He's going in a minute.

JENNY. Don't be looking at me for money.

TERRY. I'm not here for money. I'm here to see my mother.

JENNY. She's in there well.

TERRY. What way is that to talk?

BRENDA. It's very late, we're all a bit stressed so just tell me what it is that you need and I'll try my best to sort it out for you.

TERRY. I told you I just wanted to see my mum.

BRENDA. She was awake; you woke her up, so why did you stay in here if you really wanted to see her?

TERRY. Because I didn't want her to see me.

JENNY. That makes a lot of sense.

TERRY. I've gone long enough without seeing the people that I love. Sometimes I just want to see them – look at them – watch them.

JENNY. Dead on.

TERRY. You wouldn't understand. You're too young.

JENNY. I'm not too young for anything.

BRENDA. Let me check and see if she's asleep.

TERRY *waits while* BRENDA *checks.* RITA *is asleep and so* BRENDA *returns.* TERRY *goes in and sits watching* RITA.

Let's get back to bed.

JENNY. Wait until he goes.

BRENDA. I'll wait for him you need your sleep though I don't know why.

JENNY. What's that supposed to mean? I'm always getting woke up in the middle of the night.

BRENDA. Well here's your big chance to get to sleep.

TERRY *gets restless.* JENNY *turns the TV on.*

If you're going to stay up, do something useful.

JENNY *sits on the settee.* BRENDA *reaches* BABY *towards her.*

JENNY. I need a break from this Mummy. I'm just going to watch one programme. Can you not keep her in with you tonight?

BRENDA. Why don't I just move the cot into my room and keep her with me permanently?

JENNY. Do you want to?

BRENDA. No, Jenny I don't.

BRENDA *goes into the kitchen to check on the tea.* TERRY *returns to the living room.* TERRY *takes money out and reaches a couple of notes towards* JENNY.

TERRY. Take the baby upstairs and give me a chance to talk to your mum.

JENNY. Where'd you get that?

TERRY. I knew you were going to say that. What happened to you kid?

JENNY. Where did you get it?

TERRY. Never mind where I got it. I don't think you look like a person who can afford to mind where I got this money from.

JENNY *takes the money.*

JENNY. I'll go up but I'm not taking the baby.

TERRY. That was the deal.

BRENDA *returns with two cups of tea.* BRENDA *hands a cup to* TERRY.

JENNY. Where's my tea?

TERRY. Brenda, we have to talk love.

BRENDA. There's a drop left in the pot if you want it.

TERRY. I need a place to stay.

BRENDA. Well you can't stay here.

JENNY *goes into the kitchen.*

TERRY. I'll make up a bed down here.

BRENDA. It wouldn't work. Things are hard enough.

TERRY. What's the point in us paying rent for two houses when I could just stay here until I get on my feet? You know it makes sense. Two TV's. Two cookers. We can't afford it.

JENNY *returns with her tea.*

JENNY. We've our own TV and cooker.

TERRY. That's what I'm saying.

JENNY. They're not yours.

TERRY. I know they're not mine. Keep your voice down.

BRENDA. It really wouldn't work.

TERRY. Tell you what. I'll just stay tonight and that will give you time to think it over. One night? After all I've done – you can't find it in your heart to give me one night on your settee.

BRENDA. One night.

JENNY. You can't, Mummy. You're not thinking properly.

TERRY. Jenny, sometimes you really think you want to say something to somebody but then later you find out something about that person and you really wish that you hadn't said what you said but it's too late and you just feel bad.

BRENDA. We'll talk in the morning – let's get this wee one to bed.

JENNY. What's Mark going to say?

BRENDA. Bed Jenny.

TERRY. Who's Mark and what would it matter what he would have to say about anything?

BRENDA *glares at* JENNY *unhappy at her bringing* MARK *into this.* JENNY *regrets it immediately.*

JENNY. I'm away on up.

BRENDA. I won't be long behind you.

JENNY *kisses* BRENDA *goodnight.* BRENDA *and* TERRY *wait for* JENNY *to leave.*

TERRY. Who is this Mark character?

BRENDA. A friend.

TERRY. No such thing.

BRENDA. I'm not going to get into it with you. He's a friend now drop it.

TERRY. How many times have I told you Brenda a man can't be friends with a woman – it doesn't work like that.

BRENDA. Never mind.

TERRY. Platonic is that what they call it well let me tell you what platonic means. It means the woman won't let the man into her knickers but the man thinks it's worth putting up with all her shite long enough to get another chance at it. That's all it is and if this guy Mark is spinning you bullshit about being friends take it from me he's only after one thing and one thing alone.

BRENDA. Well he's not so...

TERRY. He's not what? You're confusing me here.

BRENDA. He's not my friend.

TERRY. What is he then?

BRENDA. He's my partner.

TERRY. Partner – as in business partner? Let me tell you something, a man can't be in business with a woman unless he's a loser – and even if he is a loser he can't be deliberately and solely in business with a woman because all that loser is thinking about is having dirty office sex.

BRENDA. Where do you get this from?

TERRY. I know about men.

BRENDA. Not everybody is the same as you.

TERRY. That's right they're not – there are no gentlemen like me left. Don't you forget I waited until we were married – how many men can you say that about?

BRENDA. Why am I talking about this?

TERRY. I'm only trying to protect you.

BRENDA. Well don't. I've been alone here without your protection for a very long time.

TERRY. Without my protection – is that what you think?

BRENDA. God help me – you are really annoying me and I can't help it but if I don't go to bed now I might say some things.

TERRY. Marky Mark Taggart? Is that who it is?

BRENDA. I'm not playing your game.

TERRY. He likes wee boys and Mark Playfair is a baldy wee shite. Is it one of them?

BRENDA. It's none of your business.

TERRY. Mark McKnight – is it him? You've always liked him?

BRENDA. I'm not even going to respond because you are just going to go through the yellow pages and I can't stand it when you get like this. I really have to get some sleep because that little baby is going to be waking all of us up again in another couple of hours.

TERRY. Mark…I don't know any more Marks. Who is he?

BRENDA. Good night.

TERRY. Mark Goodnight?

BRENDA. You've been working on that sense of humour yet you're still not funny.

TERRY. There's no such thing as a good Knight. The age of chivalry is dead don't fall for his bullshit. What yarn is he spinning you? Down on his luck is he?

BRENDA. He's not down on his luck.

TERRY. Doing well for himself then? What's he do?

BRENDA. He's got a job and a house and a car if that's what you want to know. Happy?

TERRY. I'm happy for you. I mean that and I wish the both of you all the things that I couldn't get for you. I hope he looks after you and treats you well.

BRENDA. I'll tell him you said that.

TERRY. You know no matter how much shit we put each other through I always have it deep in my heart that one day we'll be back together.

BRENDA. I didn't know you had a heart.

TERRY. I deserved that. I deserve a lot of things but just tell me this. This guy is he the end for us? I mean, is this the special one, the replacement, the new me?

BRENDA. What time are you getting up at?

TERRY. Early, I'll be away early.

BRENDA *leaves* TERRY *alone.* TERRY *takes the money from his pocket and counts it. It totals £280.* TERRY *is delighted. The door is tapped very gently.* TERRY *goes to the door.* HEATHER *enters the living room, wearing her jogging suit and fluffy pink slippers, with* TERRY *following her obviously trying to stop her going too far.* RITA *hears them and sits up to listen.*

HEATHER. I knew I would find you here.

TERRY. Keep your voice down.

HEATHER. I waited for the lights to go out.

TERRY. Why?

HEATHER. Because I knew that you were still here.

TERRY. I'm staying here.

HEATHER. Where?

TERRY. Lower your voice. I'm staying down here.

HEATHER. You're trying to get back with her.

TERRY. She won't let me get back with her.

HEATHER. She's letting you stay here.

TERRY. Only for one night.

HEATHER. Yeah, yeah, that's how it always starts.

TERRY. You better go before she comes down.

HEATHER. Kiss me.

TERRY. Don't start.

HEATHER. If you kiss me I'll believe you. I'll know you haven't any feelings for her left and then I can head on home and let you finish whatever wee scheme you have in your head.

   RITA *doesn't want* TERRY *to kiss* HEATHER.

RITA. Who is that? Who's in there?

TERRY. See what you've done.

HEATHER. You do still have feelings for her don't you?

RITA. Is that you Terry?

TERRY. Yes Mum.

HEATHER. What about us? Are we...finished? Not that it's a big deal to me. I'd just like to know.

   BRENDA *enters the living room.*

BRENDA. What are you doing here?

HEATHER. I'm here to see him.

BRENDA. What about?

TERRY. We're friends.

BRENDA. Friends? (*Laughs.*)

TERRY. I owe her money.

BRENDA. He doesn't have any money, Heather.

HEATHER. Well then maybe he can pay me in a different way then.

BRENDA. What's that supposed to mean?

TERRY. Have you got a few quid you could just give her to get rid of her?

HEATHER. Get rid of me? Who do you think you're talking about?

BRENDA (*to* TERRY). Go and see your ma.

TERRY *hesitates before he goes in to see* RITA. BRENDA *and* HEATHER *look at one another.*

HEATHER. This is like one of those moments isn't it?

RITA (*to* TERRY). Sit with me until I go back to sleep son.

TERRY *sits beside the bed.*

BRENDA. What are you really doing here, Heather?

HEATHER. You don't want him any more, Brenda. So what do you care who does?

BRENDA. You come here to see my husband under my roof.

HEATHER. He's not your husband anymore and even if he was what would you do about it?

BRENDA. Get out of my house before I do do something about it.

BRENDA *moves towards* HEATHER *and* HEATHER *is overcome with fear.*

HEATHER. I'm only messing with you, Brenda. It's like he says, he owes me money and I've been looking everywhere for him. I mean who would have thought he would come here, eh? Fuck sake. Can't even take a joke any more.

BRENDA *goes for the money and discovers it is missing.* BRENDA *goes upstairs.*

Terry? Terry, come here.

TERRY *is unsure what to do.* RITA *holds his hand to prevent him leaving.* BRENDA *returns and gives* HEATHER *some money.*

BRENDA. That should be enough to get you through the night.

HEATHER. Thanks. (*To* TERRY.) Terry?

BRENDA. What do you want him for you got what you came for?

HEATHER. Tell him I'll need the rest tomorrow.

HEATHER *leaves.* TERRY *waits.* BRENDA *waits.* RITA *lets go of* TERRY*'s hand.* TERRY *goes into the living room.*

BRENDA. Where's my Christmas money?

TERRY. I knew you were going to say that.

BRENDA. Well where is it then? I need it to get everybody their presents this weekend.

TERRY. I have it. I didn't want her to find it. You know what she's like.

BRENDA. Who? Your friend?

TERRY. She's not my friend.

BRENDA. You said she was.

TERRY. That's cause she was standing there.

TERRY *gives* BRENDA *the money.* BRENDA *counts it.*

I knew you would do that.

BRENDA *goes to put the money back where it was then looks at* TERRY. TERRY *smiles at her.* BRENDA *wonders how safe the money would be and then decides to test* TERRY. BRENDA *places the money where he can see it.*

You know after what I did for you I thought, hoped, you could find it in your heart to let this thing with Heather go? It was one time and I never meant it to happen. After sixteen years in prison a man has needs…those needs can get out of control and make a man do things. Some people say time heals but time can also be cruel – look what it's done to us.

BRENDA *walks out of the room.* TERRY *goes to bed.*

Scene Four

TERRY *wakes in the living room.* BRENDA *is sitting with*
RITA. BRENDA *is dressed.* RITA *is in her nightclothes.*
BRENDA *feeds* RITA *her eggs and toast as she sits up in bed.*
BRENDA *is also rocking the pram gently.* BABY *is sleeping.*
GAIL *and* HEATHER *arrive at the door.* TERRY *allows them*
into the room. GAIL *is wearing a different denim outfit and is*
swamped in jewellery. HEATHER *is in the same jogging*
bottoms and pink fluffy slippers.

HEATHER. Where's Brenda?

TERRY. I don't know, I've just woke up.

GAIL. You weren't sleeping with her then?

TERRY. What do you want?

HEATHER. The rest of the money you owe me for a start.

TERRY. I don't owe you any money.

GAIL (*calls*). Brenda.

   BRENDA *enters the living room.*

   Good, you're up. We need you to come with us.

BRENDA. It's very early. Can I get changed?

HEATHER. You're dead on like that.

   JENNY *enters with a cup of tea.*

RITA. Who was at the door?

BRENDA. Nobody Rita. Jenny will you finish that for me?

JENNY. Where are you going?

BRENDA. A message.

JENNY. Can I not come with you?

BRENDA. No you can't.

JENNY. I can't stand this; you never let me do anything.

GAIL. Hey! Jenny, remember that chat we had about respect.

JENNY. Do you like my jacket? I want to come with you.

GAIL. It's great. You can come with us tonight if your mum's agreeable.

JENNY. Where are we going?

BRENDA. I won't be agreeable so forget about it.

BRENDA *notices that* JENNY *is dressed very similar to* GAIL.

TERRY. Brenda?

BRENDA. You won't be here so what does it matter to you. (*To* JENNY.) Finish the breakfast and help Rita wash her own...bits and pieces.

JENNY. I'm not doing that.

BRENDA. How long are we going to be?

GAIL. It depends on how it goes.

JENNY. Why can't he do it?

BRENDA. Leave it. I'll do it when I come back. Take that jacket off it doesn't suit you.

JENNY. It does. I just need a few things to go with it. (*To* GAIL.) Where'd you get that necklace?

GAIL. In the Rangers shop obviously.

BRENDA. You're not going out so you don't need a jacket.

HEATHER. I better go in and get a jacket.

GAIL. There's no time. You can go like that.

BRENDA. Her next bottle is in the microwave already. Just heat it up.

GAIL. It's her baby Brenda. She knows what to do. Don't you?

JENNY. Of course I do but she always gets on like this. Do you want to go into town with me later on?

GAIL. We'll see what happens.

HEATHER. Can I even just run in and put my fighting boots on? In case there's trouble.

GAIL. Hurry up then!

HEATHER *leaves.*

JENNY. She's a header, isn't she?

GAIL *studies* JENNY *and thinks about* HEATHER*'s ineptitude and how it might damage her own prospects.*

BRENDA *(for* TERRY*'s benefit).* She's an idiot.

TERRY *(for* BRENDA*'s benefit).* Ugly too.

JENNY. A ten pinter.

TERRY. Twenty pinter more like.

GAIL. That's funny, she was good enough for you on Monday night and I don't remember you having twenty pints.

TERRY *(to* BRENDA*).* That's not true.

BRENDA. You did have twenty pints then?

TERRY. No, you know what I mean.

GAIL. You're a liar. Why are you getting on like that?

TERRY. I'm not a liar. She is.

BRENDA. Is she?

GAIL. She's a lot of things but she's not a liar.

TERRY. Well if she's saying anything happened between me and her on Monday night then she is a liar. I went with her that one time when I was out of my mind, which by the way I had to be to go anywhere near her. But I haven't been near her ever since. I swear on my life.

GAIL *(to* BRENDA*).* You know her Brenda. If she says they slept together again – they slept together again.

TERRY. This is my house you're standing in and that's my wife you're talking to.

GAIL. Put me out of it then.

TERRY. If you weren't a woman.

GAIL. You mean if you weren't a woman.

TERRY *freezes completely uncertain as to what to do next.*

BRENDA. Did you not say we had to be somewhere, Gail?

GAIL *stops glaring at* TERRY *and glances at* BRENDA. BRENDA *guides her eyes to* JENNY *indicating that she doesn't want* JENNY *to hear this.* GAIL *understands.* BRENDA *leaves with* GAIL. JENNY *sits immediately and begins to flick through the channels.* TERRY *watches her.*

TERRY. What are you doing today?

JENNY. I'm going back to bed in a minute.

TERRY. Well what are you doing in general? What's your plans?

JENNY *stands and tosses the remote control towards* TERRY.

JENNY. You watch whatever you want.

TERRY. Are you going to tidy this place like your mum asked you?

JENNY. I've a million things to do not just this. If I get round to it I get round to it. There's nothing stopping you doing it you know.

TERRY *folds up the blanket and puts the pillow on top of it.* TERRY *goes and looks in on* RITA. RITA *is sleeping.* TERRY *lights a cigarette.*

TERRY. Do you want one?

JENNY. My ma doesn't allow me to smoke.

TERRY. Your ma's not here.

JENNY. True. (*Takes the cigarette and lights it up*).

TERRY *takes out his wallet and opens it.* TERRY *shows* JENNY *some photographs.*

That's me. Oh my God look at the state of me.

TERRY. Lots of times in your life I'm sure you thought I was shit because I wasn't there but this was my way of sort of being there. That one there is your first day at school. And that one was your first school play.

JENNY. Did my mummy give you these?

TERRY (*nods*). See sometimes you think a person doesn't care because they're not there but sometimes a person just can't be there no matter how much they want to.

JENNY. Are you staying here all day? Did my mum say you could?

TERRY. Do you think I should?

JENNY. Is that you and my mum?

TERRY. We were a great couple weren't we?

JENNY. You look good together.

TERRY. That's where you get your looks from our kid. I mean it. You're a great-looking girl – a real heart breaker.

JENNY. I wish.

TERRY. How could any daughter of mine not be? (*Pause.*) Maybe I should have a wee chat with your mum about how grown up you are. You're old enough to smoke if you want to. You're old enough to make up your own mind about a lot of things. Do you drink?

JENNY. My mummy doesn't allow me but when I'm out I have a couple.

TERRY. You see, you seem responsible enough to me. I have a slight advantage over your mum, because she was here the whole time with you she still thinks of you as the wee baby that couldn't walk. The wee baby that she had to teach how to walk, and talk and eat and burp and go to the toilet. She got to be with you through all the great things that

I missed. But, being away I didn't see you as a helpless little baby or a careless little girl. You seem all grown up to me but your mum probably has too many memories of you being helpless or falling over or getting yourself in trouble. (*Stands.*) I'd love to chat here all day but I have to get going.

TERRY *gets up and pretends he is going to leave.*

JENNY. Where are you going?

TERRY. One night only – remember?

JENNY. What are you going to do?

TERRY. Maybe a wee café will be open and I could scrounge a cup of tea off somebody.

JENNY. Don't be scrounging.

TERRY. Is that embarrassing for you? I never meant to be like this you know.

JENNY. I'll get you some lunch when I finish this. Sit down and tell me about you and my mum. My mum never talks to me about stuff like that.

TERRY. Things could've been so very different if it had been up to me.

JENNY. Why don't you get money from the UDA? Gail says that they always look after their own.

TERRY. Maybe they do but sometimes they don't.

JENNY. Gail says if you do time for them you get serious money. Like those guys that come out and end up living in big houses in the country. Why don't you do that?

TERRY. It's complicated.

JENNY. I'm not thick. Don't treat me like that. I can understand things when they're explained to me.

TERRY. I don't know what people told you when I was away or what your mum said.

JENNY. She told me you were the greatest guy in the world.

TERRY. Did she really?

JENNY. Yeah, but then today she said she made that up to protect me because I was young.

TERRY. I can't talk about this. Your mum should've told you.

JENNY. You tell me then.

TERRY (*pause*). Tell me what you know.

JENNY. I know that just before I was born you killed a man for the UDA. He was in the IRA and you became a hero but you had to go to jail.

TERRY. Is that what you believe?

JENNY. That's what I was told but I don't see any of the money the other heroes are getting.

TERRY. First of all it wasn't a man. It was a woman.

JENNY. An IRA woman?

TERRY. They said she was.

JENNY. You didn't know and you killed her anyway.

TERRY. I didn't know and I didn't kill her.

JENNY. I don't believe this. Why are you telling me this?

TERRY. You said you wanted to know the truth.

JENNY. Then tell me the truth. Not that you were set up that you didn't really kill her.

TERRY. I didn't say I was set up. I pleaded guilty.

JENNY. So you did do it.

TERRY. No I didn't.

JENNY. Why did you plead guilty then?

TERRY. Your mum had just found out that she was pregnant with you and we weren't exactly loaded and things weren't exactly going very well if you know what I mean so we decided – I decided – that it was for the best.

JENNY. So you just stepped up and said you did it. 'It was me', and off you went to prison for like twenty years. That is the stupidest thing I've ever heard. Did you do it for the money? Did they give you money when you were inside?

TERRY. I did sixteen years, from when your mum was pregnant until a couple of months ago and I didn't do it for money. I didn't get any money.

JENNY. What did you do it for then?

TERRY. For you.

JENNY. How for me?

TERRY. Because you needed your mum here.

JENNY. You're not making fucking sense to me.

TERRY. Don't swear.

JENNY. Then don't treat me like a kid and I won't have to.

TERRY. You are so like your mum right now. Standing up trying to make yourself look taller.

JENNY. I'm tall enough.

TERRY. Don't try to be too tall like your mummy did.

JENNY. Why what did my mummy do?

TERRY. Let's put it this way when your mum was a wee girl . . . not a wee girl . . . about your age I mean. She was like a raging bull. She had a temper. She was always trying to prove herself. Always trying to prove she was old enough to drink and smoke and fight and...

JENNY. Did my mummy drink and smoke when she was my age?

The doorbell sounds.

TERRY. Who would that be?

JENNY. Mark.

TERRY. Your mummy's Mark?

JENNY (*moves towards the door*). Yeah, he's doing the fireplace.

TERRY. That's who he is. Wait!

JENNY. What?

TERRY. Let me get upstairs before you let him in. Then when he's in say you have to go to the shops or something and leave him here to me.

JENNY. What are you going to do?

TERRY. Do you want your mum and dad to get back together or not?

JENNY *considers this and then allows* TERRY *to sneak upstairs before she lets* MARK *into the house.* MARK *enters and prepares for work.*

JENNY. I've to go to the shops Mark will you be all right?

MARK. I'll just work away. Where's your mum?

JENNY. She had to go out a message.

MARK. Will you be as quick as you can? You know what your granny's like if she wakes up and I'm the only one in the house.

JENNY *leaves.* MARK *walks very quietly into the kitchen and returns with his tools.* MARK *checks on* BABY *before returning to work on the fireplace.* MARK *stops what he is doing when he hears* TERRY *singing from upstairs.* MARK *is upset at this noise and begins to panic when he hears footsteps coming down the stairs.* TERRY *enters the room wearing only his boxer shorts and carrying his clothes.*

TERRY. You're keen, starting work this early.

MARK. I promised her I'd have it finished for Christmas.

TERRY. I know, I know all about it. Got to have everything done in a certain way by a certain time. My wife is a real slave driver. (*Begins dressing himself.*) I remember when they were letting me out of prison I says to one of the big guards, 'Have you any idea what you're letting me in for when I get home?' and he laughed his balls off. But there's a truth in that. When I first got out and came here it was worse than being in prison. She runs it well like, the house, don't get me wrong I'm not complaining about her, whatever she wants she wants you know what I mean? But! These things have their limits.

MARK. What are you actually doing here Terry?

TERRY. I know you've been getting close with her and all that so it's good that you're the first to know. We're going to give it another go.

MARK. When did this happen?

TERRY. Last night. We just sat up talking and sorting things out. Now, we didn't sort out everything but you never do, do you?

MARK *is devastated but attempts to hide it well and goes back to work.*

RITA. Who is that talking out there? Brenda? Terry?

TERRY *goes to the door.*

TERRY. It's only the guy that does the fires. He won't be long.

RITA. Don't leave me here with him on my own Terry love.

TERRY (*to Mark*). What do you reckon half an hour finish that off? (*To* RITA.) Half an hour Mum.

RITA. That's good love. I don't like strangers in our house.

TERRY *walks away from the door.*

TERRY. Any wee bits that needs tidied up I can do over the weekend mate. So don't be thinking you have to work your balls off. I know my wife can ride you really hard and I'm not talking about the bedroom here I mean with work. Get this done, get that done. Just between me and you and these four walls she can ride you really hard in the bedroom too. Last night. Oh boy, the things she did for me, blow your mind.

MARK *fumes and has to work very hard to not lose his temper.*

RITA. Terry?

TERRY *goes in to see* RITA.

Terry love, are you all right?

TERRY. Of course I am. Why, do you need something?

RITA. No, I wanted to make sure that you were OK that's all. I feel like I haven't seen you for a while. Sit beside me.

TERRY *sits beside the bed.* RITA *watches him for a while.* TERRY *has nothing to say to his mother.*

Do you need anything? You know you can always come to me no matter what it is, I'm here and I always will be for my little boy. I got something for you.

RITA *reaches under her bed and takes a little box out. She opens it and takes some money from inside and gives it to* TERRY.

This is for you. I've been putting a wee bit away each week you know in case you needed something. I know it's not much.

TERRY *takes the money.*

Have you got a hug for an old woman?

TERRY *hugs* RITA.

TERRY. I better get in and keep an eye on this guy. You know what workmen are like.

RITA. Watch him close Terry and if he gives you any trouble give him a good wallop.

TERRY *returns to the living room and begins to watch TV while* MARK *works.* MARK *finishes up as quick and loud as he can.* TERRY *cannot seem to concentrate with the noise.*

TERRY. There must be somewhere you would rather be than here. That's good enough for me besides once I'm on my feet I might get it all ripped back out again and put it back the way it was.

MARK *gathers up his tools and leaves the place in a mess.*

Does she still owe you something?

MARK. No, it's all clear.

TERRY. She always was good with money, always looked for bargains. I would prefer something to be done properly, professionally you know but she would prefer the cheapest. Kept me right that way but that's only one reason I married her. The other was of course you know what. And after all these years she still hasn't lost it. Oh, last night man, you should have seen her.

TERRY *begins to illustrate when* MARK *barges by him with his tools.*

MARK. I got to go.

TERRY *enjoys watching* MARK *leave in a rage.* TERRY *returns to the TV.*

RITA. Who's that?

TERRY *ignores* RITA.

Who's that? Brenda? Terry? Is that you?

TERRY. It's me Mum.

RITA. Terry? Come in and let me see you.

BABY *wakes and begins to cry.* TERRY *stands immediately and goes to the pram.* TERRY *tries to rock the pram.* BABY *continues to cry.*

TERRY. She said there was a bottle already made up in the microwave.

RITA. Where is she?

TERRY. She's gone out somewhere. Mum, can you do something?

RITA. Lift her over to me.

TERRY *lifts* BABY *and gives her to* RITA. RITA *cradles* BABY *in her arms.*

I feel like I haven't seen you for a while. Sit beside me.

TERRY. I have to go.

RITA. Sit down beside your old mum for a minute.

RITA *reaches under the bed and brings out the box again.* TERRY *decides to sit.* RITA *watches him for a while.* TERRY *considers his options.*

Do you need anything? You know you can always come to me no matter what it is, I'm here and I always will be for my little boy. I got something for you.

RITA *opens the box and takes some money from inside and gives it to* TERRY.

This is for you. I've been putting a wee bit away each week you know in case you needed something. I know it's not much.

TERRY *thinks very carefully about his next move.* TERRY *studies* RITA *to see if this is genuine and then takes the money.*

Have you got a hug for an old woman?

TERRY *hugs* RITA.

TERRY. I better get in here I have to finish this fireplace. That worker guy didn't do a very good job – hopefully I'll be able to fix it up a bit.

RITA. That's her fault Terry, I told her to wait and let you do it. It's a man's place to take care of business. When women get involved it always turns out wrong.

TERRY. God bless you Mum.

TERRY *kisses* RITA *on the forehead.* RITA *is overwhelmed and cries.* TERRY *leaves her rocking* BABY *and goes all the way out of the house.*

Scene Five

RITA *is sleeping.* BABY *is crying in the cot beside the bed.*
BRENDA *enters and leaves all the doors open as she makes
her way into the room and places several Christmas presents
on the floor.* BRENDA *nurses* BABY *and places her in the
pram after closing the doors.* BRENDA *begins to sort out the
presents and wrap them.*

RITA. Is that you Terry?

BRENDA. No, it's me.

RITA. Where's Terry?

BRENDA. Out.

RITA. Who's in?

BRENDA. Just me and you and the baby.

RITA. What baby?

BRENDA. Go back to sleep or pretending to be asleep
whatever it is you were doing when the baby was crying.

RITA. I can't hear you.

BRENDA. You never can when it suits you.

RITA. I'm hungry.

BRENDA. Rustle us up a sandwich then.

RITA. What?

BRENDA. Cheese and tomato for me please and you can have
whatever you like.

RITA. I can't hear you, what are you saying?

BRENDA (*louder*). I'll get you something in a minute.

RITA. What time is it?

BRENDA. Time you got off my back.

RITA. I'm not on your back.

BRENDA. That's not what I said.

RITA. I heard you.

BRENDA. You can't hear me from in there, your hearing isn't good enough remember. Oh no you can't 'cause your memory's gone too.

RITA. I can hear what you're saying. What did you say?

BRENDA (*louder*). I said I don't know what time it is I just got back.

RITA. Have you not got a watch on?

BRENDA. No, like everything else in this house it doesn't work.

RITA. What about the lovely watch that Terry bought you?

BRENDA. Like Terry it was cheap and broke all the time.

RITA. What?

BRENDA (*louder*). If I make you a cup of tea will you stop shouting? I've just got her to doze off.

RITA. I don't want a cup of tea I just want something to eat.

The door is banged and BRENDA *goes to it and opens it.*

BRENDA. I'll be one minute I'm just getting her a drink.

GAIL *and* HEATHER (*now wearing her fighting boots and jeans*) *bring* ADELE *into the living room and wait.* ADELE *is wearing a tight top that covers very little of her body and a very short skirt and stilettos.* BRENDA *brings* BABY *back into* RITA*'s room and gets* RITA *a drink.* BABY *begins to cry again.*

RITA. If I have to drink I want a real drink.

BRENDA. You don't drink, Rita and I don't have time for your memory to come back so just trust me on this one and take the water.

BRENDA *gives* RITA *the drink and quickly picks up all the presents and takes them out of the room.*

HEATHER. That would crack me up. Having to listen to that noise all the time.

GAIL. So, don't get pregnant then.

ADELE (*mumbles*). No chance of that happening.

HEATHER. What did you say?

GAIL. This isn't the time to make enemies.

HEATHER. What did she say to me?

GAIL (*to* ADELE). Sit down.

ADELE. I'm not sitting here listening to that.

HEATHER. You're going to be sitting through a lot worse.

GAIL (*to* ADELE). Don't start. (*To* HEATHER.) Heather?

HEATHER. What?

GAIL. Can you?

HEATHER. No way. She'll be in, in a minute.

GAIL. Come on.

GAIL *moves to the door and looks in.* HEATHER *follows her over.* ADELE *sees her chance and tries to ease herself, slowly and quietly, towards the front door.*

HEATHER. Can you sort this out, Mrs?

RITA. She'll quieten down in a second if you would keep quiet.

BRENDA *comes down the stairs and stops at the door.* BRENDA *realises that* ADELE *has managed to move very carefully, undetected, to the door.* ADELE *glares at* BRENDA *unsure what to do.* BRENDA *closes the door.* GAIL *looks into the room and sees* ADELE *close to the door with* BRENDA *blocking her way.*

BRENDA. They'd only find you and bring you back.

ADELE *follows* BRENDA *into the centre of the room.*
BRENDA *goes on through and gets* BABY. RITA *acts*
frightened.

RITA. Is that you, love?

BRENDA. Could none of you lift her?

RITA. Who are you talking to?

BRENDA. I'll have to sort this out Gail.

GAIL. Try and sort her out before Maureen gets here would
you?

BRENDA. I'll see what I can do.

HEATHER. Is there a present for me under this tree?

BRENDA *takes* BABY *into kitchen.*

RITA. Brenda, who is that out there?

BRENDA. We're just having a quick meeting, Rita.

RITA. Does Terry know about this? What time is it?

BRENDA. Just lie back down and sleep.

ADELE. Can we get this over with?

HEATHER. What's your rush?

ADELE. Things to do. People to see.

HEATHER (*rummaging through some presents under the tree*).
Listen to your woman. (*Rattles a present.*) Sounds like
chocolates to me.

BRENDA *returns with* BABY.

GAIL. Brenda, where's Jenny? Why's she not here?

BRENDA. I don't know. Look, she'll be settled in two
minutes. Besides Maureen's not here yet.

GAIL. Can you phone her or something?

BRENDA. I'll be two seconds.

BRENDA *leaves with* BABY.

HEATHER. Should have just given her to her granny.

ADELE. Why don't I go and meet you later?

HEATHER. What do we look like to you?

ADELE. I wouldn't like to say.

HEATHER. What?

GAIL. Heather, don't let her do that to you. (*To* ADELE.) You! What were you told?

HEATHER. Let's get started, we can fill Maureen in when she gets here.

GAIL. Wait on Brenda and then we'll see.

HEATHER. Can granny Mush in there not even make a cup of tea?

RITA. Who is that?

GAIL. She's an old woman, bed ridden in case you haven't noticed.

ADELE. You two are fucking dickheads.

HEATHER. What did you just say?

ADELE. Acting fucking big and talking fucking shit. I'm away.

HEATHER *grabs at* ADELE *and they begin to struggle.*

GAIL. Heather, what are you doing?

HEATHER *grapples with* ADELE. GAIL *tries to position herself to get a clear dig at* ADELE.

HEATHER. She's got my hair. I'm going to kill her.

RITA. What's going on out there?

RITA *tries to get up.* BRENDA *rushes down the stairs as quick as she can holding a baby monitoring device.* HEATHER *and* ADELE *have each other by the hair.* GAIL *is forced into action by the situation when* RITA *and* BRENDA *both arrive.* GAIL *punches* ADELE *in the kidneys. This stuns* ADELE. *As* ADELE *wobbles from the force of the blow* BRENDA *grabs* HEATHER *and pulls her back away from* ADELE *who is now down on one knee holding her back.*

HEATHER. Get off me you bitch.

GAIL. Calm down, Heather. (*To* BRENDA.) Let her go.

BRENDA. I can't let her go. She's going to do something to that wee girl.

HEATHER. Let me go.

GAIL. She won't. Let her go.

BRENDA *lets go.* HEATHER *moves towards* ADELE *who is still stunned rubbing her back in pain.* ADELE *is crying.* GAIL *stops* HEATHER *in her tracks.*

Sit over there. (*To* BRENDA.) Get your mum back in bed.

BRENDA *moves to* RITA.

RITA. Get these people out of my son's house.

BRENDA *eases* RITA *back into the room and* RITA *climbs into bed.* GAIL *kneels beside* ADELE *and talks calmly.*

GAIL. I don't want to hurt you. I don't even want to be here but I have to so I'm going to ask you this favour. Make this as easy for me as possible, do what I say and we'll be out of here before you know it.

BRENDA *waits for* RITA *to be comfortable and then returns to the living room.*

Do you understand me Adele?

ADELE. It's her.

GAIL. Forget about her. Just listen to me.

ADELE. OK. Just keep that slag away from me.

HEATHER. Who are you calling a slag?

GAIL. I'm going to help you up.

GAIL *and* BRENDA *help* ADELE *onto the seat.* HEATHER *stays back. Door bell rings.*

BRENDA. Are you all right, love?

GAIL. Go and get the door Heather.

> HEATHER *goes to the door reluctantly.*

BRENDA. You have to keep her under control, Gail.

GAIL. I can handle it.

> JENNY *enters with* HEATHER. JENNY *has bought jewellery to replicate* GAIL*'s image.* BRENDA *is unhappy with this development.*

BRENDA. Get upstairs.

JENNY. What's happening?

HEATHER. We're having a wee chat with this wee bitch here.

BRENDA. Up the stairs.

JENNY. I want to see this.

BRENDA. What did you let her in here for?

HEATHER. It's her house.

GAIL. Jenny, go and check on your daughter.

JENNY. But Gail…

GAIL. Do it.

> BRENDA *watches in amazement as* JENNY *goes out of the room.*

HEATHER. Let's get this started, Gail. Something must have happened to Maureen.

GAIL. OK. Open in prayer.

ADELE. You're fucking joking me.

HEATHER. Let's just get on with it; Maureen's not here.

GAIL. Close your eyes. (*To* BRENDA.) Brenda you say it. Keep it simple.

ADELE. Unbelievable.

GAIL. Close your eyes, bow your head, show some respect and you might get out of this in one piece.

ADELE *realises the seriousness of her predicament and closes her eyes.* GAIL *watches* ADELE *for a second, checks* HEATHER, *who pretends to close her eyes and then bows her head.* BRENDA *watches everybody.*

BRENDA. Thank you lord. And please help us all here today to do the right thing.

HEATHER *lifts her head and sees that* ADELE *has her eyes open.* HEATHER *slaps her in the head.*

I'm praying here.

GAIL *lifts her head.* ADELE *jumps to her feet.* GAIL *separates them.*

GAIL. The next person who interrupts this prayer will really wish they hadn't.

GAIL *pauses and waits until she believes she has their commitment.*

HEATHER. Are you saying that to me? She had her eyes open.

GAIL. How'd you know that?

HEATHER. I checked on her.

GAIL (*to* BRENDA). Go ahead, Brenda.

BRENDA. God forgive us for doing this.

ADELE *searches quickly for something to use as a weapon.*

God give us wisdom to know what is the right thing to do and the courage to do it if we have to.

ADELE *hits* HEATHER *in the side of the head with an ornament.* HEATHER *goes down injured.* BRENDA *grabs* ADELE *and pushes her back onto the seat.*

GAIL. You have really fucked yourself.

ADELE. She started it.

BRENDA. Don't make things worse.

RITA. What's going on out there?

BRENDA. Nothing. Go back to sleep.

ADELE. I'm being threatened.

GAIL. Shut up.

RITA. Did you say threatened? By who?

GAIL. Have you any smelling salts 'cause she's out cold.

ADELE. Don't leave me here on my own.

BRENDA. I'm just going to the kitchen.

> BRENDA *goes to the kitchen.*

ADELE. Phone the police Mrs. They've taken me hostage and are going to kill me.

RITA. Who is that Brenda?

BRENDA. Don't worry about her. She's just a kid.

RITA. Who's going to kill her?

BRENDA. Nobody. Go back to sleep.

> JENNY *enters the room.*

JENNY. Oh my God, what have you done?

GAIL. Give me a hand with her will you?

ADELE. She hit me during prayers. You must have seen it.

JENNY. You're so dead.

RITA. Who is that, Brenda?

BRENDA. It's nobody, we're just having a wee meeting.

RITA. What kind of meeting.

BRENDA. A prayer meeting.

> BRENDA *returns to the living room.* GAIL *and* JENNY *have moved* HEATHER *to the sofa.* ADELE *has moved to a seat near the door.* BRENDA *uses the smelling salts on* HEATHER *who wakes up immediately and is very angry.* GAIL *indicates that she is not allowed to hit back.*

HEATHER *feels very sick.* BRENDA *rushes back to the kitchen.*

Don't let her be sick on my floor.

HEATHER. Give me something.

GAIL. You're all right.

ADELE. Don't be sick on me. Get her away.

BRENDA *rushes back in.* HEATHER *is sick on the floor before* BRENDA *can get to it.* BRENDA *gives* HEATHER *the basin.*

HEATHER. Can I have some tissues or something?

JENNY. I'm going to be sick too.

GAIL. Just look away.

BRENDA. Get a mop, Jenny.

JENNY. I'm not touching it.

HEATHER *sits with the basin on her lap.* HEATHER *motions to rub it into the carpet with her foot.* BRENDA *prevents her.* BRENDA *keeps the door open and gets a mop.*

HEATHER. It's all her fucking fault.

GAIL. She'll be dealt with in time. She's already fucked herself, don't copy her example.

ADELE (*shouts towards* BRENDA). You saw her hitting me, Brenda, didn't you?

HEATHER. She was praying, she didn't see a thing.

GAIL. Is that the only reason she didn't see it?

HEATHER. What do you mean?

GAIL. Try, it didn't happen, that's how she didn't see it.

HEATHER. She's fucked either way.

BRENDA *returns with some wipes and gets on her knees to clean the mess.*

JENNY. I heard it through the baby monitor. She hit Heather when her eyes were shut.

ADELE. Can you fucking see through this baby monitor?

JENNY. Oh aye, you know what I mean.

BRENDA. Stay out of it.

JENNY. She can't get away with it.

BRENDA. You can't prove it.

JENNY. Heather always has her eyes closed for prayers, isn't that right Gail?

BRENDA. How would Gail know? Her eyes are always closed.

HEATHER. They'll never be closed again after that I'll tell you that for nothing.

GAIL. Drop this now. (*To* JENNY.) Jenny, go up and get the baby.

JENNY. Let her sleep.

GAIL. Then go up and see to her. (*To* BRENDA.) Brenda, stay with the old lady?

JENNY *leaves the room in a bad mood.*

ADELE. And leave me in here with these two that wasn't the deal?

BRENDA. I can leave the door open.

BRENDA *checks on* RITA.

I'm just closing this door over, Rita.

RITA. That's all right. I've already said my prayers.

BRENDA *leaves the door ajar and sprays the room with air freshener.*

HEATHER. That's going to make me sick again.

BRENDA. Use the basin.

GAIL. OK. Prayers are over. Let's get down to the first order of business. Did you get the books and files and everything else yet?

BRENDA. There's people here.

GAIL. What of it?

BRENDA. I don't want people to know what I do.

GAIL. It's not illegal.

BRENDA. That's not the reason.

HEATHER. What's your problem then?

BRENDA. I just don't want people to know my business.

GAIL. She's not a thief.

ADELE. I never stole anything in my whole life.

GAIL. I just said that.

HEATHER. That's probably a lie.

GAIL. Just answer the question. Do it in code if you like.

BRENDA. All right, I've got everything and it's in order, it's been checked.

HEATHER. And has the money started coming in OK?

BRENDA. Code.

HEATHER. Fuck!

GAIL. What was in those smelling salts?

ADELE. I don't care what you're talking about anyway. I like you Brenda, I'm not going to do anything or tell anybody anything. I've always liked you.

GAIL. So?

BRENDA. Yes, the 'stuff' has…the money has started coming in. Everything is fine.

GAIL. Let me know immediately if there are any problems.

HEATHER. You gave away the code not me.

BRENDA. What?

HEATHER. She didn't know it was money until you told her I gave the code away.

BRENDA. You gave the code away.

HEATHER. You told her that I had given the code away that was how she knew.

GAIL. Drop this. You're doing my head in.

HEATHER. Think about it I could have been using money as a code word for something else.

BRENDA. Money is not a code word it is money. Money means money. Nobody uses a code word like money.

HEATHER. That's what could've been so clever about it. She's thick. She wouldn't know that.

ADELE. I'm not thick.

HEATHER. I could've used money as a code for bread or dough. Think about it.

BRENDA. I think that blow to the head has really damaged you.

HEATHER. You're not listening. Any word can be a code. Anything can mean anything if it has been agreed beforehand which by the way it wasn't. Am I right Gail? I could've meant drugs or goods or anything.

GAIL. Let's just drop it.

HEATHER. Are you taking her side?

GAIL. I'm not taking sides. Second order of business. Adele, you've been accused of encouraging suspected IRA men into our area, supplying them with information and setting up contacts for their friends. How do you plead?

ADELE. Plead? This isn't a court.

HEATHER. How do you plead?

GAIL. Is this a picture of you with an IRA man?

ADELE (*laughing*). That's my boyfriend.

HEATHER. He's in the IRA.

ADELE. No he's not.

GAIL. You witness this, Brenda. Adele has identified herself as being the person in this picture. Agreed?

BRENDA. Her boyfriend looks like a wee lad to me.

GAIL. That doesn't matter.

HEATHER. Wee fenian bastard, that's what he is.

ADELE. You're a bigot.

HEATHER. No I'm not, I just hate taigs.

GAIL. Do you bring the man in the picture into the estate on a regular basis?

ADELE. He comes up to see me.

HEATHER. Why don't you go to his stinking hole of an estate and see him there?

ADELE. In spite of the obvious appeal you've just mentioned I don't go there because I'm not allowed in his estate.

GAIL. Why do you think that is?

HEATHER. You shouldn't want to go to his fucking estate.

ADELE. Brenda, can you believe this?

BRENDA. Answer the questions and we can get this over with quickly.

ADELE. What was it again?

GAIL. You know what it was.

ADELE. I'm not allowed in his estate.

GAIL. Then I asked you why do you think that is?

ADELE. Because I'm a protestant obviously.

GAIL. That's correct.

HEATHER. And that's why he's not allowed in this estate.

ADELE. Hello? He's not a protestant.

GAIL. You know what she means.

HEATHER. You think you're fucking funny don't you?

GAIL. He's not only a catholic but he's a suspected IRA man.

HEATHER. Maybe that's why you can't get any Prods to go out with you.

ADELE. I don't want any Prods to go out with me.

GAIL. Hey, stay with me here.

ADELE. I'm trying to but she keeps interrupting.

HEATHER. She keeps being smart.

ADELE. Maybe that's why I can get a nice catholic fella to go out with me.

GAIL. From now on nobody else speaks but me.

HEATHER. Anybody can get a catholic fella, they're easy.

ADELE. You can't.

GAIL. Shut up both of you. Only speak when spoken to by me.

HEATHER. It's her.

GAIL. Heather?

ADELE. You can't even get a dickhead Prod from this shithole.

HEATHER. Who's talking now?

GAIL. Let me explain something here. I take this very seriously but I'm getting the impression that I'm the only one, so let me tell you what I'm going to do. The next person who interrupts me or disrespects me in any shape or form is going to be very, very sorry. Am I clear here?

GAIL *waits and nobody speaks.*

We've established that this guy is your boyfriend and we've been informed and are informing you again that he is a suspected IRA man. Do you have anything to say before I continue?

ADELE. Can I speak now?

GAIL. Obviously when I ask you a question you can speak.

ADELE. OK. Know the way that you said that I wasn't allowed in their area because I was a protestant and then you said he wasn't allowed in our area because he was a catholic yeah?

GAIL. What's your point?

ADELE. The point is that you are always saying we are better than them, so how are we if we just do what they do?

GAIL. Fair point now let me explain it to you. You're not allowed in their area solely because you are a protestant. That's the only reason do you admit that?

ADELE. I don't know I just don't go in case there's trouble.

GAIL. And why would there be trouble?

ADELE. Trouble can start for millions of reasons.

GAIL. Your parents don't allow you to go up there. I know this is true because your dad runs you everywhere, he even runs you to the shop and that's only a hundred yards away. The reason he doesn't run you up The Falls is because he knows like we know that The Falls is not safe for protestants.

ADELE. Same as Rathcoole isn't safe for catholics.

GAIL. You're wrong and if you'd let me finish you'd understand better.

ADELE. Go ahead.

GAIL. Catholics are not only allowed in Rathcoole but they are actively encouraged to come here, to live here, to socialise here.

ADELE. Then how come my boyfriend is being threatened?

GAIL. Your boyfriend is at this moment in time a suspected IRA man. That is why some of the men in the UDA are worried not only about him coming here but also about him seeing you. Unlike The Falls where they would rape you and kill you as soon as they found out you were from here the men of Rathcoole have not done that to him, in fact they've tried to help him. They didn't touch him. They didn't intimidate him. They merely tried to protect him by telling him he can't come here while he is under suspicion of these offences against our community.

ADELE. He's not in the IRA.

GAIL. Once that is proven then he can come here as often as he likes.

ADELE. You can't prove something like that.

GAIL. Of course you can.

ADELE. What happened to innocent until proven guilty?

GAIL. Listen to me. We have friends in the Police checking him out. Now if it turns out that he is in the clear and as you claim he is not a member of the IRA then we move to the second charge that he is getting information for the IRA.

ADELE. I don't know anything so how can he?

GAIL. Has he ever asked you questions about the UDA or someone in the UDA?

ADELE. No.

GAIL. Are you sure?

ADELE. Positive, we've no interest in any of that shite.

GAIL. So he hasn't said to you one time, what about that guy or that guy is he in the UDA? Or he's never asked you if you or your family are in the UDA?

ADELE. I told you we don't talk about things like that.

GAIL. That's hard to believe.

ADELE. It's the truth.

GAIL. If I was a catholic and I came into Rathcoole to go with a girl the first thing I would want to know is – is any member of that girl's family or circle of friends in the UDA or the UVF or any protestant organisation. What do you say Brenda?

BRENDA. It would make sense if the boy asked you just to make sure for peace of mind.

ADELE. I want it on record that I didn't go for the obvious joke there.

GAIL. What joke?

ADELE. About you being gay, when you said if you were going with a girl.

GAIL. Are you disrespecting me?

ADELE. No, that's my point. If I was disrespecting you I would have gone for the joke.

GAIL *punches* ADELE *in the side.* ADELE *is stunned.* GAIL *punches her again very hard on the opposite side.* ADELE *keels over but* GAIL *grabs and holds her head still.*

GAIL. From now on you will answer my questions immediately. Clearly and completely, got it?

ADELE *nods, tears begin to flow.* HEATHER *smirks and laughs.* GAIL *gestures that* HEATHER *should be quiet.* HEATHER *covers her mouth.* BRENDA *is annoyed and concerned.*

BRENDA. The quicker you answer these questions, the quicker we can all go home.

GAIL. Has he ever asked any questions about the UDA or any member of your family or close circle of friends?

ADELE. He might have but only for the reasons Brenda said.

GAIL. Did you give him the information?

ADELE. I told him my family weren't connected.

GAIL. Did you tell him who was connected?

ADELE. No.

GAIL. You've never been walking down the street and seen somebody and maybe you quickly suggested changing direction and he said, 'Why?' and you told him that a couple of UDA fellas were walking towards you? Has that ever happened?

ADELE. No.

GAIL. Has anything like that ever happened?

ADELE. No.

GAIL. What about when he was approached by the UDA and asked who he was and what he was doing here what did you tell him about that?

ADELE. They told him they were in the UDA and that's when they asked him to leave.

GAIL. Did he ask you if that was true?

ADELE. I don't know what you mean.

GAIL. Yes you do. Did he ask you something like, 'Those guys said they were in the UDA, are they?' Did he say something like that?

ADELE. Probably.

BRENDA. This all seems reasonable, Gail.

GAIL. You don't know what we're dealing with Brenda.

BRENDA. Anybody would ask that.

GAIL. Maybe, but did he go on to ask you for their names?

ADELE. No.

GAIL. He didn't? Not even out of curiosity?

ADELE. No.

GAIL. Did he even ask you if you knew them?

ADELE. This doesn't mean anything.

GAIL. It does, Adele, just keep answering the questions.

ADELE. Brenda said anybody would ask something like that. It's natural.

GAIL. Has he ever asked you anything about the police?

ADELE. No.

GAIL. What about your Uncle John?

ADELE. He doesn't know him.

GAIL. How do you know that?

ADELE. They've never met.

GAIL. Are you aware of how dangerous it is for your uncle if it turns out this guy is in the IRA?

ADELE. But he's not.

GAIL. He might be giving them information for all you know.

ADELE. He's not.

GAIL. You don't know that. Has he tried to bring his friends into the estate?

ADELE. One of his mates used to go with a girl from here.

GAIL. What happened?

ADELE. She packed him in.

GAIL. Give me the names.

ADELE. Tracy Sheen and his name was Cairan Mcsomething.

GAIL. Are you aware that this guy Cairan McIlhatton was in fact in the IRA and that's why she no longer sees him or lets him come into the estate?

ADELE. No.

GAIL. Has your boyfriend never told you this?

ADELE. He told me he was threatened and that's it.

GAIL. And what happened?

ADELE. He got scared and never came back.

GAIL. Has your boyfriend ever asked him to come back or asked you to let him come back?

ADELE. No.

GAIL. So you've never set up another date with say a girl called Rachel from your snooty university?

ADELE. That was just a stupid thing. She was having a party and he didn't want to come on his own so he brought his mate and they ended up going together and then having a row because he wouldn't have sex with her in the house.

GAIL. Who told you that?

ADELE. He did.

GAIL. And you believed him?

ADELE. Why would he lie about not having sex?

GAIL. Because he's a bloke.

HEATHER. Because he's a catholic.

BRENDA. Can I say something here?

GAIL. Do you want to ask a question?

BRENDA. Yeah.

HEATHER. How come she gets to ask a question?

GAIL. Go Brenda.

BRENDA. Do you love this guy?

ADELE. What do you mean?

BRENDA. It's a simple question. Do you love him?

HEATHER. What's this got to do with anything?

GAIL. Let her answer.

BRENDA. If you love this guy with all your heart. I mean truly, deeply, with every fibre of your being. If you are willing to give up your life for his then I need to know about it right now. Is this guy the one? Does your heart race when you see him? Does it miss a beat when you kiss? Is there ever a moment in the day when you don't think about him?

ADELE. We've only been seeing each other for six months.

HEATHER. Six months too many.

GAIL. So six months is too soon to fall in love with a man but not too soon to have sex with him?

BRENDA. Forget about him. He's not the one.

ADELE. I'm not forgetting about him just because you say so.

HEATHER. She's not the only one saying so.

BRENDA. This might seem really cool to you. All this attention that you're getting but let me tell you something you don't know. See this woman here (*Heather*) she would do anything to get ripped into you. And the only reason she doesn't is because this woman (*Gail*) won't let her.

ADELE. I'm not afraid of them.

BRENDA. Listen to me. This isn't a game. If they decide that you are guilty they are going to shave your head, strip you naked, pour hot tar all over you and roll you in feathers. And believe me it only gets worse after that.

ADELE. Fuck this.

HEATHER. No, fuck you bitch.

GAIL. You should listen.

ADELE. You can't touch me. My uncle's in the police.

BRENDA. Then go and talk to him. Tell him what's been said here and tell him that you don't even love this guy.

ADELE. Are we done?

GAIL. I think so.

HEATHER. What about me?

GAIL. Are you done Brenda?

BRENDA. There's nothing else I can say.

HEATHER. What about me I said? Why can't I ask her a question?

ADELE. Can I go or not?

BRENDA. If you love this wee lad you won't ask him to come back and if he loves you he won't come back anyway.

ADELE. I'm out of here.

HEATHER. Are you just going to let her go?

> ADELE *walks out of the house.* GAIL *stops* HEATHER *from following her.*

GAIL. We've to report this to Maureen. Let her know we got what we wanted even if it did take longer than I thought. FYI (*for your information*) Maureen doesn't need to know about any of that shit that happened earlier. As far as she's concerned everything went smoothly.

HEATHER. We've to find out why she wasn't here anyway.

BRENDA. Maybe she wanted Gail to see what it would be like to be on her own with something like this.

GAIL. You're good Brenda. You should do this full time.

BRENDA. I was just trying to help the kid.

GAIL. If you did this sort of thing for me when I take over maybe it wouldn't seem like I was doing it on my own.

HEATHER. Hey, you weren't on your own. I did my bit too.

> JENNY *comes into the room.*

JENNY. I heard the door, what happened?

BRENDA. Never you mind.

RITA. Is that you, love?

> BRENDA *goes to* RITA.

BRENDA. You're all right. It's just some people going.

RITA. I want a drink. Not that diet stuff a proper drink.

> BRENDA *goes for a drink.*

GAIL. You should have seen what your mum done there, kid.

JENNY. What?

GAIL. You should really listen to her. She's very smart.

JENNY. She's not that smart. Look where she ended up.

GAIL. And are you not smart?

HEATHER. Yeah, you're not exactly a million miles away from her.

JENNY. I'm different. My whole life is still ahead of me.

HEATHER. That could be very short if you don't learn some stuff, like that wee bitch we were sorting out before you came down.

JENNY. Did you sort her out in the end?

HEATHER. Of course we did.

> BRENDA *returns with a drink and gives it to* RITA.

We better get going. Can you run me down to the offy Gail?

JENNY. Can I come with you?

HEATHER. No, we've to meet…some people.

GAIL. Wait here with your mum. She's a lot to do.

JENNY. But I want to come with you.

GAIL. I'll make you a deal. If you help your mum for me, and she tells me that you did, then you can come with us tomorrow night.

JENNY. What are you doing tomorrow night? Going to the club?

GAIL. Only if you do what your mum tells you.

JENNY. It's a deal.

Scene Six

JENNY *and* TERRY *are wrapping Christmas presents.*
BRENDA *is doing her books.* TERRY *cannot stop looking at*
the money every time BRENDA *counts some.*

JENNY. Who are these wee t-shirts for?

BRENDA. They're for your cousin Peter.

TERRY. Why are you buying things for them when you never
    see them?

BRENDA. They'll send stuff for the wee one.

JENNY. What about me?

BRENDA. Presents for the wee one are for you, Jenny.

   JENNY *almost sticks* TERRY*'s fingers to the present.*

TERRY. Watch the fingers.

   JENNY *sticks his fingers anyway.*

   I knew you were going to do that.

JENNY. I take it this one is for your woman.

BRENDA. That's your grandmother. Don't be disrespectful.

JENNY. Who do you want me to write it's from?

TERRY. All of us.

JENNY. Will I, Mummy?

BRENDA. It's from me.

JENNY. What did I get her?

BRENDA. You tell me.

JENNY. This.

BRENDA. If you write it you contribute towards it.

JENNY. I will.

BRENDA. When and with what?

JENNY. As soon as my money comes through.

BRENDA. The dole must have gone up an awful lot if you're going to pay for everything that you say.

JENNY. I don't have to pay it all at once but.

TERRY. It's Christmas, Brenda.

BRENDA. I know it's Christmas.

TERRY. What's that money there?

BRENDA. Never you mind about this money.

TERRY. You could lend her some of that until her money comes through.

BRENDA. That's not my money to lend.

TERRY. You could borrow it. Put it to some good use.

JENNY. Mummy, do you think we could?

BRENDA. No.

TERRY. Brenda, when do you have to hand that in?

BRENDA. I'm not getting into this.

TERRY. Think about it. It's Christmas time. Nobody is expecting this money, not all of it anyway.

BRENDA. You've no idea what you're talking about.

TERRY. Have we not done enough for them people?

BRENDA. Have I not done enough for you?

TERRY. No argument from me about that. But I've done stuff too.

JENNY. He's not saying keep the money or steal some of it. He means use it now and pay it back later.

BRENDA. Like you do with me.

JENNY. I am going to pay you back.

Door is knocked. BRENDA *waits and then gathers up all the money, places it in a box and goes to the door carrying it with her.*

TERRY. What did you get your mum?

JENNY. Nothing yet, she won't lend me the money so how can I get her something?

TERRY. There's always a way. Leave it with me and I'll see what I can do.

BRENDA *returns with* MARK. BRENDA *goes on through and tries to be quiet.* MARK *watches* TERRY *and* JENNY.

JENNY. There's a present here somewhere for you, I think.

MARK. That's all right.

TERRY. How's it going?

MARK. Same old story really.

TERRY. Did somebody else give you the elbow?

MARK. I'm only here to get my gear not to have a conversation.

TERRY. Hey, you're in my house, be more respectful.

TERRY *stands.* JENNY *stands excitedly.* BRENDA *returns with the gear.*

BRENDA. What are you doing?

JENNY. I was looking for the present you got Mark. Where is it?

JENNY *and* TERRY *look for it.* BRENDA *looks at* MARK. MARK *looks at* BRENDA *and then* TERRY. MARK *collects his gear.*

When did you give him the elbow, Mum?

BRENDA. I didn't.

JENNY. What are you going to do then, Mum?

BRENDA. That's none of your business.

TERRY. I'll tell you what she's going to do, love. She's going to wake up on Christmas Day and she's going to realise that Santa left her a family for Christmas.

JENNY. Are you going to let my daddy move in permanently?

TERRY. We'll see what happens.

JENNY. Mummy I told you if you let my dad stay Mark wouldn't like it so when you think about it you only have yourself to blame.

BRENDA. Things will sort themselves out.

JENNY. It's not right. I can't stand this.

TERRY. What's wrong with you?

JENNY. This. Not knowing what's going to happen. One minute we're a family and the next we're not.

BRENDA. And who's to blame for that?

TERRY. There is no blame.

BRENDA. There is. You are. You chose to sleep with that whore; no one made you do it. You did it; you wanted to do it.

TERRY. I just got out of prison. Sixteen years without…doing it can leave a man vulnerable. You don't know what it was like.

BRENDA. How do I not? What was I doing all that time?

TERRY. Are you saying in all that time you never had another man? Do you really expect me to believe that?

BRENDA. Why don't you ask her?

JENNY. She didn't, Daddy.

TERRY. Ask my daughter if I'm a liar.

BRENDA. Ask your mum.

TERRY. What about him?

BRENDA. I haven't done anything with him.

TERRY *glares at* MARK. MARK *remains silent.* TERRY *throws the presents down.*

TERRY. I'm not listening to this.

BRENDA. Go round and see if your whore will let you stay with her for Christmas.

TERRY. You'd love that so as you can move him in here behind my back.

BRENDA. I could've moved him in any time.

TERRY. Why didn't you?

BRENDA. Because I'm not like that. Though sometimes I wish I was.

TERRY. Don't ever say that.

BRENDA. Go on out.

JENNY. Don't Daddy, stay and help me do this.

TERRY. I'm not leaving until he does.

BRENDA. I got you something for Christmas. You might as well have it now.

JENNY. What is it, Mummy?

BRENDA *goes to her set of drawers and takes an envelope from the top.* BRENDA *gives it to* TERRY. MARK *becomes excited.*

TERRY. What is this?

BRENDA. A present; money can't buy.

TERRY *begins to look in the envelope.*

TERRY. Just tell me what it is.

BRENDA. It's your freedom. Take it and go.

TERRY. Do you really want me to?

BRENDA. I'm saying it.

TERRY. Say you don't love me any more and I'll go.

BRENDA. I don't have to say that. I thought it was obvious.

TERRY. Humour me. Just pretend I need to hear it.

BRENDA. I want you out of my house. I want you out of my life. I wish I had never met you.

TERRY. That's a terrible thing to say in front of Jenny.

BRENDA. She needs to know the truth.

TERRY. Nobody needs to know that their mother wishes they weren't here.

BRENDA. Don't twist my words. You're the one I wish wasn't here.

TERRY. What about my mum are you going to throw her out on the street too? Or put her in a home.

BRENDA. What do you care?

TERRY. That's my mum you're talking about.

BRENDA. Then take her with you if you care so much about her.

TERRY. You know I can't do that.

BRENDA. Why not?

TERRY. I don't have any money. Where would we go? Where would we live?

BRENDA. Tell you what – stay here. I'll go. How does that sound?

TERRY. Go and live with this Whoremaster? Over my dead body.

BRENDA. That can be arranged.

TERRY *rushes towards* BRENDA. BRENDA *doesn't budge.* JENNY *jumps up and screams.* MARK *stands.* RITA *pretends to wake.* TERRY *stops.*

TERRY. Relax. I'm not going to do anything.

BRENDA. No change there.

RITA. What's going on?

TERRY. Nothing Mum.

MARK. Maybe me and you should take this outside.

TERRY. Any time you're ready mate.

RITA. Is that you Terry?

TERRY. Yes Mum, I'm just leaving.

BRENDA. I'll get you your tea in a minute just hang on.

RITA. Terry, come in and let me see that you're all right.

TERRY. I can't.

BRENDA. He doesn't want to.

   TERRY *raises his clenched fist.*

TERRY. Shut up.

MARK. Watch it.

JENNY. Keep out of it.

BRENDA. Tell her the truth.

TERRY. I'll tell you the truth. I've never hit a woman in my entire life but you are coming very, very close to it.

BRENDA. Go ahead and see what happens to you.

TERRY. Are you threatening me?

RITA. What's happening?

TERRY. I wouldn't waste my energy on you. You fucking whore.

MARK. Don't call her that.

   TERRY *turns and walks towards the door.*

BRENDA. You're mixing me up with her.

TERRY. If the name fits.

   BRENDA *throws an ornament towards* TERRY. *It narrowly misses.*

   That could've hit me.

BRENDA. Didn't you know I was going to do that?

RITA. What was that noise?

TERRY. Jenny go and tell her everything is all right.

BRENDA. Do it love.

RITA. Terry? Brenda?

BRENDA. Two seconds and then I'll take over. Before she wakes the wee one.

JENNY. I can hear you.

JENNY *leaves the room.*

TERRY. I'm going to go here and I might not come back.

BRENDA. Do you think that I'm going to react to that, breakdown or something?

TERRY. I'm serious this time.

BRENDA. Music to my ears.

TERRY. Forever is a long time to wait on somebody.

BRENDA. I won't be waiting for you if that's what you think.

TERRY. What happened to you?

BRENDA. How many ornaments do I have to break before you get the message?

TERRY (*to* MARK). I'll see you later.

BRENDA. Is that supposed to scare him or something?

TERRY. He knows what it means.

TERRY *leaves.*

BRENDA. You should maybe wait a minute before you leave.

JENNY *comes back in.*

JENNY. What happened?

BRENDA. He's gone.

JENNY. Mummy, no.

BRENDA. It's a good thing.

JENNY. Maybe for you but what about for us?

BRENDA. He would only end up letting you down sooner or later. He's not the guy you think he is.

JENNY. Why can't you give him a chance, just one chance?

BRENDA. Because I can't. Every time he goes out the door I wouldn't know where he was going. Every time he kisses me I wouldn't know who he was kissing.

JENNY. One mistake.

BRENDA. One mistake is all it takes, Jenny love. Once a man is unfaithful…disloyal to me or to you, that's it – that man can never be loyal or faithful again. (*To* MARK.) You can go now, he wouldn't have waited that long.

MARK. I could stay for a while.

JENNY. He's a-scared (*afraid*).

MARK *studies* BRENDA. BRENDA *gets the books and goes back to work.* JENNY *waits.* MARK *leaves with his gear.* MAUREEN *enters the house and waits at the door to the living room.*

MAUREEN. The door was open.

BRENDA. What is it?

MAUREEN. I want to talk to you.

JENNY. I know, I know.

JENNY *gets up and leaves the room.* BRENDA *listens to the doors closing before offering* MAUREEN *a seat.* MAUREEN *sits.* BRENDA *hangs her coat up.*

MAUREEN. I'll make this as short and sweet as possible. I need a favour.

BRENDA. This is every time I see you now, Maureen. I'm starting to feel like maybe it's not so good to see you coming.

MAUREEN. That's why I'm giving it all up. I have to because it's got like that with everybody. Even my own family cringe when they see me coming.

BRENDA. That's terrible.

MAUREEN. Comes with the territory but not for much longer.

BRENDA. Then you understand why I want out too, don't you?

MAUREEN. There was a meeting, Brenda. To discuss my replacement and I nominated Gail and thought no more of it – normally at county level I get my own way, they like to let each district leader look after their own – but it wasn't as simple as that.

BRENDA. I know; there's a trial period or something.

MAUREEN. No. They don't want Gail.

BRENDA *feels sick.*

She's not the friendly, sociable, politically-correct face that they want. She scares people. She scares most men for flip sake.

BRENDA. You always need a strong leader, especially one who could stand up to the men.

MAUREEN. No, they won't let it happen.

BRENDA. Can't they let everybody vote?

MAUREEN. No. The vote was taken at county level – all six of them voted for you. You have sense.

BRENDA. Do I not scare people any more? For God's sake Maureen you know what I've done – you know my history – how could they vote me over Gail?

MAUREEN. Gail hasn't changed and never will. You have.

BRENDA. Have I?

MAUREEN. Yes you have. You're unrecognisable compared to the way you were.

BRENDA. You have to speak to them. Tell them what I'm really like. You know me Maureen I'm a nasty piece of work.

MAUREEN. They liked your ideas.

BRENDA. You told them my ideas.

MAUREEN. All about the Christmas thing, they loved it.

BRENDA. Why not just go back and say they were Gail's?

MAUREEN. I can't do that.

BRENDA. I'm already doing the bookkeeping thing.

MAUREEN. You can get someone else to do that. You'll be in charge.

BRENDA. And what about Gail, you don't think she's going to be just a little bit upset. Fuck sake Maureen you promised her this.

MAUREEN. You know I don't like it when you swear.

BRENDA. And neither do they and I swear all the fucking time. Tell them that.

MAUREEN. The last thing I'm going to do for you...is tell Gail.

BRENDA. I can't believe this.

MAUREEN. This is what they want. If there was something else I could do I would do it.

Silence.

RITA. Terry? Terry love come here and let me see that you're all right.

MAUREEN *leaves.* BRENDA *looks at the presents and then her work.* BRENDA *puts her pen down and listens to* MAUREEN *leaving the house.*

Terry?

BRENDA *goes to bed.* RITA *gets up and enters the living room.* RITA *searches the living room and finds the UDA money.* RITA *takes it back to bed.*

Scene Seven

RITA *is sleeping. The house is in darkness apart from a small
table lamp beside* RITA*'s bed.* TERRY *enters the house and
comes into the living room.* TERRY *searches for the money
then hears* RITA *coughing.* TERRY *looks in on* RITA. RITA
waves him over to the bed. TERRY *sits beside her.*

RITA. Are you all right, son?

TERRY. I'm fine.

RITA. How did you get in, you're not supposed to have a key?

TERRY. Jenny leant me hers.

RITA. Is Jenny in on this?

TERRY. In on what?

RITA. She's your daughter Terry. Your flesh and blood, you
shouldn't involve her.

TERRY. I'm not involving her in anything I'm just trying
to…get to know her a bit.

RITA. It's not there.

TERRY. What isn't where?

RITA. It's really well hidden; you won't find it.

TERRY. Am I going to find out what you're talking about?

RITA. I've lost a lot of things. I lost my house, my job, my car,
my memory isn't as good, my body doesn't work like it
used to but I'm not a lost cause completely.

TERRY. I know.

RITA. If you got that UDA money – you wouldn't be able to
pay it back son.

TERRY. I would.

RITA. I know your intentions are to pay it back. You've always had good intentions son but in reality you don't have that thing that makes a person actually follow through. I blame prison.

TERRY bows his head in shame. RITA gets her tin and hands him the money.

That's why I've been saving so hard recently so as I could help you avoid these little temptations…these prison habits.

TERRY. I can't take this. I don't want to take this.

RITA. You can, you do, and you will. You've only been out a couple of months, things will get easier and easier from now on.

RITA closes his hand over the money. TERRY hugs and kisses RITA. RITA lies down and goes back to sleep with TERRY watching over her. TERRY listens to the door being knocked and decides to wait where he is. TERRY checks that RITA doesn't wake and turns the light off. BRENDA enters the living room with MARK. MARK takes a seat. BRENDA watches MARK. MARK is intoxicated in more ways than one.

BRENDA. What do you want?

MARK. Do you mean what do I want right now or what do I want long term?

BRENDA. Start with what do you want now.

MARK. A kiss.

Awkward pause as BRENDA decides not to give him a kiss. MARK is hurt.

BRENDA. OK. Let's try long term.

MARK. I thought maybe we would find that out together. What do you want?

BRENDA. Long term I just want peace and quiet. Right now I want a good night's sleep.

MARK considers this and feels lost and alone.

MARK. I should go.

BRENDA. Good.

MARK. You're a hard woman Brenda.

BRENDA. You're a drunk man Mark.

BRENDA *watches* MARK *going towards the door.* MARK *stumbles and falls to his knees.* TERRY *thinks this is an act.* BRENDA *keeps her distance.*

MARK. I don't know what to do without you. I've been wandering around all night wondering what I could do to get you back.

BRENDA. And is this what you came up with? Get drunk and fall over. What am I supposed to do about that? Fall hopelessly in love with you.

MARK. Could I come back again tomorrow if I get a Plan B?

BRENDA. Will there be drink involved in this Plan B?

TERRY *realises that* BRENDA *is weakening.*

MARK. No. I'll be clean and sober I promise.

BRENDA. I don't believe in promises.

MARK. I don't ever want to be anywhere where you're not.

BRENDA. Let's see if you feel the same way tomorrow.

MARK. I won't even go to work I'll just come here.

BRENDA. No you won't, you'll go home, go to sleep, get up, go to work and then if you still feel the same way…I'll see you here tomorrow night.

TERRY *storms across the room and attacks* MARK.

TERRY. Not on my watch.

TERRY *and* MARK *roll around the floor wrestling.* BRENDA *trails* TERRY *off* MARK. TERRY *tries to kick* MARK *as he is trailed away.*

BRENDA. Where did you come from?

TERRY. I was talking to my mum.

BRENDA. How did you get in here?

TERRY. What does it matter?

MARK *tries to get up but finds it very difficult to stand.*

BRENDA. Mark, sit down 'til I get a chance to check you're OK.

TERRY. Never show your face here again mate or you'll get worse.

BRENDA. Shut up Terry.

MARK *walks out of the house.* TERRY *breaks free from* BRENDA.

TERRY. I can't believe you. In my house, talking like that.

BRENDA. Talking like what?

TERRY. Tell my ma I'll see her tomorrow.

BRENDA. No, you won't see her tomorrow or ever again unless you arrange to meet her somewhere because you won't be getting back into this house. I mean it Terry I've had it with you. You just stay away from now on.

BABY *starts crying.* TERRY *walks out.* RITA *goes back to sleep.* JENNY *enters the living room with* BABY *in her arms.*

JENNY. I can't get her back to sleep.

BRENDA *takes* BABY *from* JENNY.

BRENDA. Did you let him in?

JENNY. I leant him my key. He needs a place to stay.

BRENDA. He needs a lot of things, Jenny. We can't help him any more.

JENNY. We can. If you just give him a chance. You owe him that much.

BRENDA. I don't owe him a thing. Did he say I did?

JENNY. No, we just talked.

BRENDA. What did you talk about? What did he tell you?

JENNY. Lots of things.

BRENDA. Specifically about the past, what did he tell you?

JENNY. He told me that he did the time but he didn't do the crime. And he also told me that he did it all for me.

BRENDA. Did you believe him?

JENNY. I don't know what to believe.

BRENDA *and* JENNY *sit.* BRENDA *places* BABY *gently in pram.*

BRENDA. Maybe I do owe him something. Jenny, your dad is a superhero. He went to prison for me because I was told by people like your new best friends who are also superheroes to go and kill a young catholic woman who was in the IRA and coming into our area to set people up and I believed them and I did it just like I believed this superhero when he told me 'til death us do part. I suppose he left that bit out as usual. See that's the thing about him, he never tells the whole story, just the part that makes him look good.

JENNY. So you killed an IRA woman. That's why Gail likes you. That's why they always come here. That's why they always want you to do stuff.

BRENDA. Why do you think I'm always telling you to have nothing to do with them?

JENNY. Unbelievable.

BRENDA. I didn't know if she was in the IRA or not. I just took their word for it because I was young and I believed them. I was a teenager like you. A real head-banger but I grew up and I learned things – like how to think for myself and look after myself and how to prioritise. I used to have a list it read like this: protestants, Ulster, the Queen, Britain and fuck everything else but I changed that list to me, my mum, my daughter and her daughter and that's the way it will stay.

JENNY. Why are you getting on like this?

BRENDA. He's trying to make you think that he did the right thing. Let me tell you what he did. He ran away from you. He didn't want me to go to prison and leave him here with you. And his mum, did I mention her? He wanted to get away from her and he wanted to get away from me and I don't really blame him we weren't a great couple obviously. But he was the great love of my life. The one and only in fact if you must know. And my other great love was my country and look how that turned out. You could say both of them have let me down.

JENNY. I can't stay here.

BRENDA. Why not?

JENNY. You're a murderer.

BRENDA. You've changed your tune. It was cool when Gail and Heather were bragging all about what they've done but when it's me it doesn't count does it? No matter what your ma does she always gets it wrong. She just isn't cool.

JENNY. I'm going.

BRENDA. You've nowhere to go.

JENNY. I'll follow him. I'll catch up with him.

BRENDA. Go to bed Jenny. We've had a really bad day.

JENNY. I can't. (*Moves to door.*) I can't just go to bed after this.

BRENDA *grabs* JENNY *and pushes her against the wall.*

BRENDA. You can fuck your life up just like I fucked mine up but I will not let you fuck this little one's life up. Do you understand me?

JENNY. She's my baby.

BRENDA. Well for the first time in your life you remembered that. Wonders will never cease.

JENNY. Let go of me.

BRENDA. Are you scared? You're trembling. Is that the thought of me doing something to you right now or is it the thought of being left alone with her?

JENNY. I can look after her. I can take her with me.

BRENDA. You can't. You can't have her. You can leave here in the morning if you want but I can't let you take her with you.

JENNY. You can't stop me.

    BRENDA *forces* JENNY *back against the wall.*

BRENDA. You really don't want to find out what I can or cannot do Jenny.

JENNY. You're really hurting me. Let me go.

BRENDA. You go up to bed and rest. We can talk properly in the morning.

    BRENDA *allows* JENNY *to go.* JENNY *rushes up the stairs.* BRENDA *turns out all the lights and sits by the door waiting, nursing* BABY. RITA *sits up in bed, waits for her eyes to get accustomed to the darkness before getting out.* BRENDA *enters her room and switches the light on.* RITA *freezes.*

    What are you doing?

RITA. I'm not staying here.

BRENDA. Let me help you back into bed.

RITA. Don't touch me.

BRENDA. You're out of your mind.

RITA. Sometimes I am and sometimes I'm not. So what? Today I'm not.

BRENDA. It's not daytime, Rita.

RITA. Don't mock me. I know what you're doing.

BRENDA. What am I doing now, stealing your money again?

RITA. Money is missing, that's true.

BRENDA. You don't have any money.

RITA. That's where you're wrong. I have my money.

BRENDA. I collect your money every Tuesday Rita, if you had any in here I would know about it and I would've kept it safe for you.

RITA. That's a joke.

BRENDA. Rita, if I wanted to steal from you I would just keep your money for myself. I don't need to do any cloak and dagger stuff.

RITA. Sometimes when you're old and bedridden people think you're worthless.

BRENDA. Don't talk like that. Have you ever heard me talking like that?

RITA. People forget about you. They forget that you're there and you can see things and hear things and feel things.

BRENDA. I'm sorry Rita if you heard all that stuff. It's just anger and frustration. It doesn't mean anything; you're old enough to know that.

RITA. I'm old enough to know lots of things.

BRENDA. I was just mad at Terry so I shouted at him and he shouted at me and that's it.

RITA. To you maybe that is all that happened but it's not. Let me tell you something you ruined my little boy's life. I saw him that first day in prison and he asked me never to come back and I looked deep into his eyes and asked him if he really did kill that wee girl and I saw it. Mothers know when their sons are lying and he lied for you and you've been living a lie ever since.

BRENDA. Let me get you back into bed this is all.

RITA. He went with that girl once. She was a whore who snared him, seduced him when he was just out of prison – I can't think of anything easier. But you can't find it in your heart to forgive him. Even after all that he has done for you. Sixteen years, Brenda.

BRENDA. I don't really need this right now.

RITA. You need help Brenda. Lots and lots of help.

BRENDA. I'm OK. I've always got by.

RITA. Not this time you won't.

BRENDA. What are you talking about?

RITA. Your money's gone.

BRENDA (*laughs and grows increasingly nervous*). What are you saying? What money?

RITA. I'm sorry.

BRENDA. You don't know what you're talking about. My money's gone. My Christmas money?

RITA. Their money.

BRENDA *goes to where she put the money and realises that it is not there.* BRENDA *contemplates the repercussions of this.* RITA *sits on the edge of her bed*

BRENDA. Are you going to tell me where it is?

RITA *indicates that she is not and climbs into bed.* BRENDA *waits at the door.*

Scene Eight

RITA *is sitting up in bed reading and listening.* MAUREEN *is in the living room with a cup of tea.* HEATHER *and* GAIL *are sitting.* BRENDA *is pacing.*

MAUREEN. We're not just under pressure from county level. We're also getting it from our own local media and from the men's divisions. So we have to be more thorough. We're always under the spotlight so we have to take extra care to get things right.

GAIL. Adele is guilty. She even attacked Heather during prayers in front of your face.

HEATHER. She has to be punished.

GAIL. It's not *just* that she's guilty. It was her whole attitude. You saw her.

HEATHER. She's a wee whore.

GAIL. Am I telling lies, Brenda? Now's the time to say.

MAUREEN. The men want something done. You know what they're like Brenda, they are going to stop these boys coming back in to our community but that's not good enough is it? They wanted to send her up to one of their punishment squads. That wouldn't be right.

HEATHER. We can do her.

GAIL. Heather shut up.

MAUREEN. Some of the men wanted to do worse than that. There are many ways a woman can be marked. Brenda, they could ruin that wee girl's life.

BRENDA. Get to the point please.

GAIL. Be careful, Brenda. You've made a mistake here.

HEATHER. Just how much money have you lost?

BRENDA. I haven't lost any money, Heather.

HEATHER. Oh yeah that's right it was stolen. Stolen right here from your house while you were asleep.

MAUREEN. I made a commitment to this organisation and the people of Rathcoole in particular many years ago when they asked me to take up the reigns of the WUDA at district level. I believe, in my time, that I have contributed to the safety and to the general well being of our community. When my commitment to this community and organisation ends I want them to remember me well. It is every abdicating leader's responsibility to hand over a tidy house at the end of their tenure. So, let me be crystal clear about what needs to happen. Brenda, you've lost a considerable amount of money. I really don't care for excuses and I'm not going to engage in some petty blame game or family squabbling. Adele has been warned time and time again and to be honest has shown a complete disregard for everything protestant. Mocked us, taunted us and upset us.

GAIL. You can clear your entire debt to us, Brenda.

MAUREEN. What do you say?

BRENDA. How far do I have to go here?

MAUREEN. Get our money's worth out of her.

BRENDA. When, where and how?

MAUREEN. Tell her Gail.

GAIL. When? Would be tonight. Where? Would be here. How? Is really up to you.

BRENDA. I have two requirements.

GAIL. You're not really in a strong bargaining position.

MAUREEN. Hear her out.

BRENDA. If I do this not only is this debt clear but my debt to this whole thing is clear forever. I want out. I want my life back.

GAIL. What else?

BRENDA. I want a declaration made that no member of my family is ever to be approached by any member of your organisation and if they take it upon themselves to approach you – you give me your word that they will be turned down for membership.

HEATHER. What about Jenny?

GAIL. She means Jenny.

BRENDA. I mean everybody.

GAIL. We can't say for men. If you have another son or if Jenny has sons that's out of our hands but if women will do then we have a deal.

BRENDA. I want to hear it from Maureen or nothing is going to happen.

MAUREEN. We have a requirement of our own, Brenda – Gail and Heather have to witness it.

HEATHER. Do you want us to bring her by?

BRENDA. No. I still need Maureen to tell me what I need to hear.

GAIL. It's not really up to Maureen any more Brenda. It's up to me and I've said yes, so can we get on with it?

BRENDA. Maureen, I need your word.

MAUREEN. I can't give it. I can go back and ask but I can't give it.

GAIL. What are you talking about?

BRENDA. Tell her. Or do you want me to tell her?

GAIL. Tell me what?

MAUREEN. There's no easy way to say this Gail. They've rejected you.

HEATHER. Fuck that.

MAUREEN. They don't think you have the necessary qualities.

GAIL. Who doesn't?

MAUREEN. I'll tell you what. Sort this out for me and I'll go back to them and explain the significance of this job and how well you carried it out.

GAIL. You gave me your word. You said you would sort this out for me.

MAUREEN. I will. Brenda wants out so I'm sure she's prepared to say that you ran the whole thing and that it went really well because of you and how you handled it. Am I right, Brenda?

GAIL. What's it got to do with Brenda? Brenda fucked up.

MAUREEN. They voted for Brenda.

GAIL. Well they'll unvote her after they hear about all the money she lost – that is if they can believe she really lost it.

HEATHER. That's right. Never mind letting her off the hook they should be doing something about her.

BRENDA. Watch what you're saying.

HEATHER. Why?

BRENDA. Gail, I know you're a little upset at the moment. This sort of news is always bad but think about it carefully. It's not over yet.

GAIL. How could they pick her? She doesn't want it. She hasn't worked for it.

HEATHER. She's not a real Loyalist. She's not a real protestant.

BRENDA. Heather, shut up.

MAUREEN. Gail, the thing is, we have to do this and you should look at it as an opportunity to prove yourself.

GAIL. Why am I on trial? I've done everything you asked me to do Maureen. Every single fucking thing – haven't I?

MAUREEN. Sometimes you can do a job too well and people want to keep you in that job.

HEATHER. They've planned this together Gail. She's always liked Brenda better than you. And *she's* always been licking round Maureen.

MAUREEN. Don't go down this road, Gail, it won't help your cause if you do something silly now.

GAIL. Here's what we're going to do – we're going to do everything like Maureen said and then Brenda you resign and nominate me.

BRENDA. Whatever makes you happy.

MAUREEN. One more thing, Gail, think about losing the baggage.

GAIL. What baggage?

HEATHER. You can't fucking trust them, Gail.

MAUREEN. That baggage.

HEATHER. Me? Are you talking about me?

MAUREEN. She was the main reason they turned you down.

GAIL. She's my right-hand woman.

HEATHER. Don't listen to her, Gail.

MAUREEN. Real leaders have to make real decisions. It's a difficult job but if you have the metal to do it…if you have the courage to take on the extra responsibility then you have to cut off whatever weighs you down. You can't afford to carry anyone, Gail.

HEATHER. Nobody carries me. (*To* GAIL.) Gail you can't drop me, I've done everything for you. These people have always been against us.

MAUREEN. Not Gail, just you. You're a mouthpiece, a blabber and a bluffer. (*To* GAIL.) And she never carries her weight.

HEATHER *walks out of the house.* GAIL *waits for a moment not sure what to do and then follows after* HEATHER. MAUREEN *moves to her coat.*

Everything is going to work itself out, Brenda.

BRENDA. I doubt it.

MAUREEN. Like I always say God works in mysterious ways.

BRENDA watches MAUREEN leave. MARK enters carrying a bunch of flowers.

MARK. I waited for all of them to go.

MARK gives BRENDA the flowers. BRENDA smells them.

I just want to say something.

BRENDA. This isn't a good time for me, Mark.

MARK. I'm not a drinking man you know that. I had three pints and I was drunk.

BRENDA. You better have something better to say than that.

MARK. I stood up to Terry last night, not very well but I did and I will do again. Those people out there they scare me but I can stand up to them too. You...you are the reason. That's all I have. I don't know if it means something to you or not but it's how I feel.

BRENDA. Timing...

MARK. I can wait. I know you have troubles and it's Christmas and I understand about Terry and the family. But I had to let you know that I'm here and I always will be.

BRENDA. That's sweet.

MARK. And if I am doing anything or have done anything that annoys you or has put you off me then I want you to know that I can change it.

BRENDA. Don't ruin it. It was nice but Mark I don't have time or energy or to be completely honest the interest right now. Why don't you find a nice girl and do this for her?

MARK. Where would I find a nice girl anywhere near here?

BRENDA. I'm sorry.

MARK is very sad. MARK leaves.

Scene Nine

In RITA*'s room* RITA *is feeding* BABY *and* JENNY *is
wrapping Christmas presents.* BRENDA *is in the living room
with* ADELE. *Sheets are spread to cover and protect the floor.*

BRENDA. I'm glad you took my advice and came round here
early. It gives us a chance to talk things over. Talk you
through your options.

ADELE. I didn't come here for that.

BRENDA. You didn't?

ADELE. No. I came to tell you to tell them to back off and
make it forever this time.

BRENDA. Do I look like a message service to you?

ADELE. You're the only one that listens.

BRENDA. Adele, it doesn't matter whether I listen or not.
They're the people you have to speak to or if you take my
advice they're the people you have to listen to.

ADELE. Well I'm not going to.

BRENDA. Calm yourself. This thing can go easy or it can
really, really hard. Sit down.

ADELE. I'm not afraid of them.

BRENDA. I've been put in charge of this. I have to tell you off
about bringing these fellas into the estate. I want you to let
me say my bit and then get yourself out of here.

ADELE. And then what happens?

BRENDA. Go somewhere where they can't find you.

ADELE. I'm staying here.

BRENDA. Then knock this fella on the head and move on with
your life.

ADELE. Why? Just because of them mouthpieces.

BRENDA. No. Because if you don't you will get hurt. What do you think happens if after today you still do what you're doing?

ADELE. I don't know.

BRENDA. They'll do you.

ADELE. They can try.

BRENDA. OK. Let's go your way. Say they do try and say you're so tough that they fail. What do you think happens after that?

ADELE. Why do you keep asking me? I don't know.

BRENDA. The men will take over. And they will do really, really bad things to you.

ADELE. Like who?

BRENDA. What does it matter who? Are you not listening?

ADELE. I don't care.

BRENDA. If this guy really loved you he wouldn't put you through all this.

ADELE. He's not putting me through anything.

BRENDA. Why don't you go and live with him where he lives?

ADELE. I'm not going to live surrounded by taigs.

BRENDA. You're going with one.

ADELE. He's different.

They hear the sound of the back door. JENNY stops wrapping and goes to the back door through the kitchen. ADELE stands and moves towards the front door. BRENDA stands beside her.

BRENDA. Think about this kid. You're dealing with two very angry women who have had nothing but disappointment in their lives. These two women are waiting for an opportunity to get rid of all their rage and frustration. Don't let them take it all out on you. Because they will, believe me they will.

JENNY *allows* HEATHER *in through the kitchen.* RITA *takes* BABY *out of pram and hushes her back to sleep.* BRENDA *goes to the front door.*

HEATHER (*to* ADELE). I didn't think you would show.

ADELE. Why not?

BRENDA *returns with* GAIL.

GAIL. Have you spoken to her yet?

BRENDA. I'm just about to. Everybody sit down. (*To* ADELE.) I'm sure you are aware of the charges against you. This meeting is to inform you that you've been found guilty as charged.

HEATHER. Now it's punishment time.

BRENDA. No. Now she has a choice. (*To* ADELE.) You can promise us faithfully now that you will end all contact with these men and we will drop the whole thing.

ADELE. Or?

BRENDA. Or we will have to take steps against you and you'll have to give him up anyway.

GAIL. So be smart. Save yourself an awful lot of trouble.

HEATHER. No, stand up to us. Make us do it the hard way.

ADELE. I'm not stopping seeing him.

GAIL. Listen to Brenda. Do what she says or we're going to have to ask Brenda to step back and forget about you.

JENNY. Adele, they have stuff in the kitchen.

ADELE. What stuff?

HEATHER. The necessary.

BRENDA (*to* ADELE). It is the pot of tar that I told you about. But it is only necessary if you refuse to do what I told you to do. Heather, help Gail to bring it in.

GAIL. I'm staying here. Jenny, help Heather bring the tar in. Unless you have a problem with that, Brenda?

BRENDA. Do it, Jenny. You should see what happens to people who don't take my advice. It might do you the world of good.

HEATHER *and* JENNY *both leave to get the tar.*

This is your last chance, Adele.

ADELE. Fuck you.

BRENDA. What did you say to me?

ADELE. You heard me.

BRENDA. Did you say 'Fuck me' in my own house?

ADELE. I'm on to you. Always pretending to be on my side. Save your bullshit for someone else.

RITA *watches* HEATHER *and* JENNY *going through with the tar.* HEATHER *and* JENNY *bring the tar into the centre of the room.* GAIL *lifts two pillows.* RITA *places* BABY *back in pram.*

BRENDA. I'm going to pretend I never heard you say that.

GAIL. Get on with it Brenda. Show us all your great leadership qualities.

BRENDA. Tell them what they want to hear and you can leave.

ADELE. All I'm going to tell you is this. You're all dead. I hope you know that.

HEATHER. Why are you going to get your IRA boyfriend to kill us all?

BRENDA. Try to see this from my point of view. I don't want to be here any more than you do.

ADELE. I'm so fucking bored listening to you. If you're going to do something, do it, if not; I have to go.

HEATHER (*to* GAIL). Are you listening to this?

GAIL. Come on Brenda, show me why they picked you instead of me.

BRENDA. Adele, you're really pushing things here. Listen to me, every time you let this guy fuck you, they feel…

ADELE. We make love.

HEATHER. You don't make love up the ass.

BRENDA. Never mind what really happens or what you think really happens. Think about what other people think happens.

ADELE. He loves me.

GAIL. He doesn't love you.

HEATHER. Every time he does you in the ass he's not even thinking about you. He's thinking about us.

ADELE. I'm not listening to this.

BRENDA. You have to listen to it.

ADELE *stands.* BRENDA *pushes* ADELE *back into her seat and indicates that* HEATHER *should speak.*

HEATHER. I knew a taig once. I wasn't a bigot until I met him and he told me that they sit in their filthy wee Irish pubs, playing their sickening wee Irish songs and imagine giving it to Paisley up the ass. And their best result is to get one of us to do it with them.

BRENDA. What do you say to that?

ADELE. What can I say to that?

BRENDA. You can say what I told you to say.

ADELE. He's not like that. He doesn't get on like that.

GAIL. You heard what she said. They're all scum. All of them. And we can't let you bring them in to our area.

BRENDA. Adele, just do it for her.

GAIL *holds her knife in front of* ADELE's *face to prevent her moving forward away from the tar.*

GAIL. Lift the tar.

HEATHER *and* JENNY *hold the tar behind* ADELE*'s head.*

BRENDA. Let her see it. Let her smell it but be careful not to spill it. She still has her last chance.

HEATHER. She better hurry up. I can't hold this up forever.

ADELE (*frightened*). Don't do it.

BRENDA. Then tell me what I need to hear.

ADELE. For fuck sake I haven't done anything wrong.

BRENDA. Tell them what I told you to say.

GAIL. Very last chance, Adele. What's it going to be?

ADELE. What ever you want just don't pour this over me.

BRENDA. Are you going to stop seeing this guy?

ADELE. Yes.

HEATHER. This is roasting.

BRENDA. Are you ever going to let him back into the estate?

ADELE. No.

GAIL. Are you ever going to let any other IRA man into this estate?

HEATHER. Or into your knickers?

ADELE. No. No.

BRENDA. Now why couldn't you have just said that at the start and saved us all this bother?

GAIL. Do it Heather.

ADELE. Get it away from me.

BRENDA. Set it down, Heather. Jenny don't!

HEATHER *and* JENNY *pour the tar over* ADELE. ADELE *screams as it burns into her hair, head and skin.* BRENDA *wrestles the pot away.* JENNY *grabs at* ADELE *copying*

HEATHER. GAIL *stabs two cushions, sets the knife on the chair and spills the feathers all over* ADELE *who is still screaming.* ADELE *struggles to her feet and runs out of the house screaming.* RITA *gets out of bed quietly and puts all the money into an envelope before returning to rocking the pram gently.* HEATHER *celebrates singing:*

HEATHER. Three cheers for the red, white and blue. Three cheers for the red, white and blue. You're a dirty fenian lover, with your dirty fenian fucker, three cheers for the red, white and blue.

BRENDA. What did you do that for?

HEATHER. It had to be done as a warning to everyone else.

GAIL. It's done now, Brenda, just leave it.

BRENDA. This is why she will always let you down, Gail.

GAIL. And is it also why your daughter will always let you down?

JENNY. Heather said no matter what happens we still have to do her a wee bit. We didn't even shave her head.

BRENDA. Get out of my sight. (*To* GAIL.) Gail, you could have done so much better. Maybe you still could but not so long as you keep shite like her around you.

HEATHER. Who are you calling shite? You're shite not me.

GAIL. Leave it Heather. We better go.

HEATHER. I'm not leaving it Gail. There's two of us and two of them. We could sort this whole thing out now. Stop them taking over. Stop them taking away our dreams Gail.

JENNY. What do you mean? Mummy!

BRENDA. You see how quickly they turn on you, Jenny? You need to understand that that wee girl out there could be you if they feel like it.

HEATHER. She's wormed her way in behind our backs Gail. She's the problem. Remember what Maureen said about when you're fighting a war sometimes you spend more time fighting your own.

BRENDA (*to* JENNY). Listen to them. This is why you should have nothing to do with them. They're just scumbags. This is nothing to do with being British. This is nothing to do with defending Ulster.

HEATHER. Listen to what she's saying. She's going to go behind our backs and blame us for this. She thinks she's better than us, Gail. (*To* BRENDA.) Don't you?

BRENDA. This is why they will never pick you, Gail. No matter what I say, no matter what Maureen says. So long as you make these kind of decisions and surround yourself with these people you will never move forward. They'll probably make me stay on to fix this now.

HEATHER. You're not better than me. You're just a whore. And not even a good one.

BRENDA. You can have my husband but you can't have my daughter. Get out of my house.

HEATHER. Fuck you. You're nothing. You're not loyal, you're not nothing. You can't keep a man satisfied. Terry told me all about you. You're useless, boring, ugly.

BRENDA *takes the knife from the chair and sticks it in* HEATHER. HEATHER *stumbles back and falls against the wall.*

JENNY. Mummy, no.

HEATHER. Gail!

GAIL (*to* JENNY). Help me get her up.

BRENDA. Leave her, Jenny.

HEATHER. Fucking bitch. Look what she did to me, Gail.

GAIL. Give me a hand.

BRENDA. Leave her, Jenny.

HEATHER. For fuck sake help me, I have to get to the hospital.

HEATHER *begins to weep.*

BRENDA. Tell Maureen I said now it's finished.

GAIL. You have really fucked yourself. This is not over by a long way.

RITA throws an envelope with the money in it onto the floor. RITA stands at the door with BABY in her arms. JENNY stands behind BRENDA looking at the knife.

What is that?

HEATHER. Help me, Gail.

RITA. Brenda messed this up and won't mind taking full responsibility for it. Heather's finished. She can go back to chasing men and keep her nose out of your affairs. You? You have behaved magnificently. I think everyone will agree with that.

GAIL checks the envelope. It is full of money.

HEATHER. Fuck sake Gail, help me.

RITA. It's all there. Feel free to count it if you have to. Jenny, help Gail take Heather out to her car. Gail, you take Heather and drop her off outside casualty and let them take care of her. Heather? You know better than to tell the police what happened here don't you?

GAIL has the money. BRENDA has the knife.

BRENDA (*to* GAIL). You want to sort this whole thing out right now just between you and me; I'm happy to do that. You want to involve other people, go and get yourself some backup; I'm OK with that too. But if you want to walk out that door and get on with your life without ever having to worry about me, let me know now that I don't ever have to worry about you and we'll call it a day and forget about each other. Because if you want to go to war with me; I'll give you a war and every single person that you ever loved, every friend you ever had and every member of your family will never ever be safe again.

GAIL considers her options.

Blackout.

The End.

A Nick Hern Book

Loyal Women first published in Great Britain in 2003
as a paperback original by Nick Hern Books Limited,
14 Larden Road, London W3 7ST
in association with the Royal Court Theatre, London

Loyal Women copyright © 2003 Gary Mitchell

Gary Mitchell has asserted his right to be identified as
the author of this work

Typeset by Country Setting, Kingsdown, Kent, CT14 8ES
Printed and bound in Great Britain by Bookmarque,
Croydon, Surrey

ISBN 1 85459 783 3

A CIP catalogue record for this book is available from
the British Library